The Nicene Creed

The Nicene Creed

Our Common Faith

EMILIANOS TIMIADIS

Foreword by Gerhard Krodel

FORTRESS PRESS   PHILADELPHIA

Library of Congress Cataloging in Publication Data

Timiadis, Emilianos.
   The Nicene Creed.

   1. Nicene Creed.   I. Title.
   BT999.T55 1983   238'.142   82–71826
   ISBN 0–8006–1653–7

9607F82   Printed in the United States of America   1–1653

Contents

Foreword

The Creed of Constantinople (A.D. 381), commonly and somewhat falsely called the Nicene Creed, was hammered out in the heat of controversy. As an expression of the church's faith, it is a communication by the church to its members on how to speak the gospel. The Creed, therefore, claims a universal, ecumenical authority, and it draws a line of demarcation between the church and heresy. The trinitarian affirmation made at Nicaea (A.D. 325) that Jesus Christ is not some demigod of popular Hellenistic religiosity and the addition made at Constantinople (A.D. 381) which affirms the full deity of the Holy Spirit constitute the basic dogma of the church—a dogma which is relevant also today because the ancient heresies of subordinationism and modalism are found in new forms and are just as false now as they were then.

The church which expressed its identity through this Creed was a Greek-speaking and Greek-thinking church. Yet the Creed is not an example of the Hellenization of Christianity, of the permeation of the gospel by the foreign ideology of the context in which the Greek church existed. On the contrary, this Creed is a milestone in the mission faced by the ancient church of Christianizing the spirit of Hellenistic religiosity and overcoming it theologically. This great task was executed by the magnificent theologians of the fourth century, men like St. Athanasius, bishop of Alexandria, and the three Cappadocian fathers—St. Basil, bishop of Caesarea; his brother, St. Gregory, bishop of Nyssa; and their friend, St. Gregory, "the theologian," who presided at the Second Ecumenical Council. The church on earth owes a debt of gratitude to these theologians. Their writings, which are accessible in convenient English editions, should also be studied by us.

As a doctrinal expression of the one faith, the Creed was received by the church under the power of the Spirit as the church's answer to particular heresies. But the Creed also became part of the church's

worship. Through its use in the liturgy it became an existential confession which united Orthodox believers especially in times of crisis
and catastrophes. The catastrophes that swept over the Orthodox
church had an intensity unknown to English-speaking Christians.
A few examples have to suffice. In A.D. 614 the Persian army conquered Jerusalem, committing unspeakable abominations on its in-
habitants and taking the holy cross to a fortress near Babylon. While
Herakleios, a Byzantine emperor, was able to defeat the Persians, to
reenter Jerusalem accompanied by the ecstatic jubilation of its people, and to reinstall the holy cross in A.D. 630, it was only eight years
later that the armies of Islam swept over Palestine, conquering Jerusalem and Antioch and three years later Alexandria as well. Thus
three of the four Orthodox patriarchates passed under Moham-
medan control. Christians became second-rate citizens burdened
with extra taxation, frequent defamation, far-reaching discrimination, and prohibition of mission together with periodic persecutions.

Another event which shocked the Orthodox church was the sack
and pillage of Constantinople by the Fourth Crusade (A.D. 1204).
The stolen treasures can be seen in Venice and other Italian and
French cities. The wantonness of these Western crusaders who
desecrated the most sacred church of Orthodoxy, the Hagia Sophia,
and the fact that a Latin patriarchate subservient to the pope was
installed, left a memory of disgust toward the Western church about
which the latter is generally ignorant.

Within the same century, the Mongols conquered Kiev (A.D. 1237)
and brought the flourishing Orthodox church of Russia to a violent
end. Even though a visitor to the Mongol court a decade later saw
only destruction, Russian Christianity was nevertheless able to
survive.

Orthodoxy was also able to survive the greatest catastrophe—the
conquest of Constantinople on May 29, 1453. In the morning of that
day, the last Christian service was held in Hagia Sophia. After re-
ceiving Communion, Constantine XI, the last emperor of Byzantium,
went to his troops and died fighting on the walls. During the eve-
ning that same day, the victorious sultan, Mohammed II, rode on
horseback into the church, which was packed with terrified people,
and claimed Orthodoxy's most sacred shrine for Islam.

The final catastrophe that broke over Orthodoxy was the Bolshevik
Revolution. Between 1917 and 1926, some seventy-five Russian bish-

ops, close to twenty-seven hundred priests, two thousand monks, and thirty-four hundred nuns and lay workers were killed. The church was deprived of the freedom of missionary outreach. The vast majority of churches were closed and desecrated. And yet today the Orthodox church in Russia is experiencing a revival in all sectors of its life. The value of a creed lies not only in its universal acceptance, but its value becomes visible in the sufferings that churches endure and in the martyrs who uphold the confession of the faith. The Orthodox churches, rich in martyrs and abundant in suffering, demonstrate the power of the Creed of Constantinople.

Confessions, being normative expressions of the church's faith, also serve as a basis for theological thought. Some brief comments may be in order on two areas where we need to hear Orthodox theologians: the issue of the *Filioque* and the doctrine of *theōsis*. Historically, some Western churches of the sixth century added the words "and the son" (Latin: *Filioque*) to the Third Article of the Creed so that the Holy Spirit in the Western tradition "proceeds from the Father *and the Son*." What began in some regional churches became the accepted notion of the whole Western church by the tenth century. It ought to be clear that the Western church had no business in tampering with the historic confession of Constantinople, and it would indeed be a good idea if the original form of the Creed were to be restored in our liturgies. With this addition, the Western church has caused much grief to the Orthodox. For instance, when the Bull of Excommunication was placed on the altar of the Hagia Sophia by the papal legate (A.D. 1045), it accused the Greeks among other things of omitting the *Filioque* from the Creed! And when the city was under Turkish attack, the Latin church refused assistance unless the Orthodox would swallow this Western addition. Moreover, we should also remember that when the Lutheran territorial churches of the sixteenth century accepted this Creed in its Western form as part of the *Book of Concord,* they did so not because they desired to enter into polemics against the Orthodox at the point of the *Filioque,* but rather because they wanted to express the continuity of the Lutheran church with the church of the fourth century.

Theologically, we should distinguish three contexts in which Western theologians have spoken of the Spirit's procession from the Father and the Son.

1. The mission and work of the Holy Spirit in history indeed pro-

ceeds from the Father and the Son. At Pentecost the Holy Spirit was given to apostles and believers by the Father through the Son, according to Acts 2:33. At this point the Orthodox and Western churches are in full agreement when the Spirit's work and mission in the church and in the world are under consideration.

2. Disagreement exists *only* at the point of the intertrinitarian relation between Father, Son, and Holy Spirit, and then only if the "procession" of the Spirit means *the cause* of the Spirit's existence. Undoubtedly, this is the meaning of "proceeds" in the Creed because it parallels the Son's being "begotten of the Father from eternity." The Orthodox, in agreement with the Creed of 381, maintain that the Holy Spirit "proceeds from the Father" alone (cf. John 15:26)— while the Western version traces the Spirit's origin and existence to the Father *and* the Son, for which there is no scriptural basis. The *Filioque* was added in Western theology because of its understanding of the principle of unity in the Godhead. Western theology held that the unity in the Godhead is constituted by the one divine substance or essence in which different relations are distinguished. This led Thomas Aquinas to equate the persons themselves with the relations. For the Orthodox the intertrinitarian relations are not the persons, but rather personal characteristics. The principle of the unity of God in Orthodox theology is found not in the one divine substance but in the *personal* principle of the "monarchy" of the Father who is the cause or the source of the Godhead and the principle(*arche*) of unity among the three. He is born of none and proceeds from none; the Son is born of the Father from all eternity; and the Spirit proceeds from the Father from all eternity.

Rightly or wrongly, the Orthodox objected to the Western *Filioque* because they felt that by locating the unity of God in the one essence, the West had turned the personal God into a theological abstraction. Moreover, they felt that the *Filioque* either introduced two principles in the Trinity (which would amount to a form of ditheism) or else the *Filioque* merged the person of the Father and of the Son so that it resulted in quasi modalism. Finally, the *Filioque* was thought to introduce the Spirit's subordination to the Son, which paved the way for Western Christomonism and for insufficient attention to the Spirit's work in the church. This in turn led to the ecclesiological misunderstanding in the West in terms of Roman institutionalism and papal autocracy on one hand and Protestant individualism on the other. At any rate the issue of the *Filioque* is an invitation to do some hard and serious trinitarian reflection which among Protestants, with few notable exceptions (for example, Karl Barth, Robert Jenson), has not happened during the past four hundred years.

3. We should also note that Orthodox theologians can speak of the Spirit's procession from the Father and the Son if procession does not mean cause, but rather *communication* of the Father's essence and energies to the Holy Spirit by the Son. Orthodox theologians in agreement with the West speak of an eternal manifestation ˙of the Holy Spirit by the Son. Moreover, each of the three persons of the Holy Trinity "dwells" in the other two. They co-inhere in such a way that only derivation ˙of origin distinguishes them, being one in essence and energy.

In the Orthodox church, the dogma of the Holy Trinity has nothing to do with Augustine's attempt to understand the mystery of God. "It is impossible to conceive God," wrote Gregory the Theologian. The dogma does not express God's mystery, but Scripture and dogma serve as guides to God, to *theōsis* which is the vision of God's glory in Christ through the power of the Holy Spirit.

Whereas Lutherans would say that the center of the gospel is God's justification of the ungodly by grace alone through faith alone, the Orthodox would locate that center in the believer's experience of deification, *theōsis*, made possible by the incarnation and the gift of the Holy Spirit. According to Athanasius "God became man that we might be made god."

While the mystery of God's *essence* remains inaccessible to all creatures, also to the glorified saints, the *energies* of God come down to us. They are the triune God's action toward humanity, his revelation, and the believers' illumination. Through his energies, God enters into relationship with people. His energies are the power of his grace which is his transforming manifestation among believers, a manifestation which is experienced by believers and called deification, *theōsis*. Among the Hesychiasts, for example, Gregory Palamas (d. A.D. 1359), the experience of God's energies takes the form of a vision of the uncreated light, the light which is God—not in his essence but in his energies. It is the light which was around Christ on the Mount of Transfiguration. A believer remains distinct from God also in his deification. He or she does not cease to be a creature but by grace, that is by God's energies, is no longer separated from God. In short, *theōsis* is participation in the life of the triune God. Its biblical basis is found not merely in isolated texts like 2 Pet. 1:4, but in Johannine and Pauline participation theology: for instance, John 17:21–23 where Christ prays that his disciples may participate in the life of God; 2 Cor. 8:9, 1 Cor. 2:12, 15–16; Rom. 8:1, 9–11; 12:1 and the formula "in Christ" and "in the Spirit." Since the middle of the nineteenth century, the relationship between justification and participation in the life of God has been one of the hotly debated issues in Pauline studies among Protestant biblical interpreters. It would seem to me that for the Orthodox, the goal of justification is sharing in the life of God, a deification which includes the whole person (1 Cor. 6:19), which begins already now but will be completed on the last day.

This book was written by an Orthodox theologian and bishop who is chairman of the pan-Orthodox delegation in the Lutheran-Orthodox dialogue sponsored by the Ecumenical Patriarchate and the Lutheran World Federation. It is an invitation to consider an Orthodox interpretation of our common Creed and to dialogue with a bishop whose daily work expresses his ecumenical commitments.

Born in Iconium, Asia Minor (Turkey), on March 10, 1917, Emilianos Timiadis lost his father (he was murdered by the Turks) in childhood. He graduated from the theological Academy Halki and served parishes in Constantinople after his ordination until 1947. He was appointed as Chancellor of the Metropolitan of Thyateira, who resided in London, and also served Archbishop Germanos and Archbishop Athenagoras until 1952. For the following seven years, he returned to pastoral ministry, working among the Orthodox of Belgium and Holland and chiefly serving Greek coal miners and seamen. In 1959 he received the degree of Doctor of Divinity from the University of Thessalonica and became a bishop. In that year he took over his present position as permanent representative of the Ecumenical Patriarchate to the World Council of Churches in Geneva, Switzerland. He represented the Ecumenical Patriarchate as observer during Vatican II and attended ecumenical assemblies and conferences. He is the author of several books published in Greek, German, Italian, French, and Spanish, among them: *Lebendige Orthodoxie* (Nuremberg 1967), *La Spiritualita Orthodossa-Morcelliana* (Brescia 1962), *Pneumatologia Orthodossa* (Bilbao 1978), *Le*

Monachisme Orthodoxe (Paris 1979), *Cosia Parla Dio* (Gribaudi, Torino 1981).

May this book by his Eminence the Most Reverend Emilianos Timiadis, Metropolitan of Sylibria, deepen our common faith, contribute to better understanding, and serve in the quest for the unity that we seek.

Gerhard Krodel, Dean
Lutheran Theological Seminary
Gettysburg, PA

Introduction

CERTAINLY THE CONFESSION of our faith in the Nicene Creed entails valuable doctrinal implications that meet the needs of all times and places. A rereading of this Creed will reveal its present-day relevance and permanent immutability, even though it is sixteen hundred years old. As is well known, the first statement of faith by the First Ecumenical Council of 325 concerning Christ's divinity and consubstantiality with the Father, which Arianism denied, was accepted by the churches of both the East and West. Yet, in spite of its reception by all, new heretics appeared and the old ones became more aggressive. Suspicious statements and confused creeds were in circulation, creating a labyrinth of frustration.[1] In view of the explosive situation, Athanasius of Alexandria, twenty years before the synod of 381 at Constantinople, warned of the need for completing the first Creed of Nicaea, considering that the doctrine of the Holy Spirit ought to be enlarged.[2]

In Cappadocia, another stronghold of Orthodoxy, Basil of Caesarea saw as dangerous the Neo-Arians, Macedonians, and Pneumatomachians, who were more keen on playing with words than on respecting the mystery of the Trinity. He therefore wrote:

> The dogmas of the fathers are despised, the apostolic traditions are weakened, the novel intentions of men become standards of policy in the church. So many, like intellectuals, technologize rather than theologize. The wisdom of this world is given the primacy over the boastings of the cross.[3]

Since it was critical that the faith be maintained in the teeth of accumulated errors, the urgent need to convoke another ecumenical council was felt ever more. Emperor Theodosius (379–95) summoned this venerable assembly in May of 381 with the participation

[1]Socrates, *Church History* (PG 67.349).
[2]*Letter to the Emperor Jovian* (PG 26.216).
[3]*Epistola* 90 (PG 32.473b).

15

of one hundred fifty delegates from the East. The sessions lasted two months, May and June. Although no one came from the West, the synod was unanimously accepted as ecumenical in 382 and was confirmed by the Fourth Ecumenical Council of Chalcedon in 451.

The fathers of the Second Ecumenical Council tried to improve and to add more elements to the basic confession of the Christian faith. A study of this fundamental text shows its clear exposition, its brief and well-chosen terms, and its variety which seek to cover the most essential areas of our faith in the shortest and most precise way. As is well known, the ancient creedal documents were written mainly for catechumens as a summary of the faith to learn and proclaim. At the beginning of the third century, homiletic and baptismal texts became so near as to complement each other. There are common features in all of them. They provide the most essential elements of faith, but at the same time they aim to distinguish the right doctrine of the church from the false and deformed teachings held by heretics.

The situation which preceded the Council was deplorable. Chaos, rivalry, abuse of secular power by the Arians, and sectarianism of all kinds were threatening the peace of the church.[4] Athanasius of Alexandria was fully conscious that the faith formulated by the First Ecumenical Council of Nicaea was not enough and that summoning a new council was urgent.[5] The same feeling was expressed by Basil of Caesarea who, though confident in the Nicene faith, expected the convocation of a new council; he did not fail to describe in the most agonizing terms the perilous situation of the Orthodox faith if efficient steps were not taken. Basil did not see the outcome because of his premature death a little before the opening of the Second Ecumenical Council (1 January 379). However, earlier he had written:

> In some places there are churches which have been entirely corrupted by falling, as it were, on blind rocks through the frauds of the heretics. Others, following the currents of the enemies of the Saving Passion suffered shipwreck in the faith . . . in some places loving admonitions ceased to operate because the love of all has grown cold. There is no Christian feeling anywhere, no compassionate tear.[6]

[4]Basil of Caesarea, *De Spiritu Sancto* I, 77 (PG 32.213).
[5]*Letter to the African Bishops* I (PG 26.1032).
[6]*De Spiritu Sancto* I, 77–78 (PG 29.213–16).

The convocation of the Second Ecumenical Council was certainly necessary and most urgent. New situations, changes in administration, and misunderstandings about the true interpretation of the faith compelled the church to refute accumulated heresies. These heresies included errors concerning God the Father, Christ, and the Holy Spirit.[7] Semi-Arians considered the Spirit as a creature, not as God or as consubstantial with the Father and the Son.[8] Moreover, such an important assembly as the Second Council gave the fathers the opportunity to consider other dimensions of the Christian faith: the resurrection of the dead and eternal life, on which the Nicene Council in 325 had said nothing. As Gregory of Nazianzus states, this Second Council complemented and improved the text of the Creed "by correcting what was imperfectly stated, since previously the matter had not been raised at all."[9]

The most fundamental issues of the Christian faith were at stake: the sovereignty of God the Father, the lordship and divinity of Christ, and the equality of the Third Person within the Holy Trinity. The Second Ecumenical Council gave attention to problems of such high importance by offering precise and clear formulations, starting with an emphasis on God's eternal origin and almighty power.

Gregory of Nyssa, not once or twice, but repeatedly in his sermons and in other writings, also presented a sad picture of the church's situation before the Council. But it was Gregory of Nazianzus who perhaps suffered most from these upheavals. He was left alone in Constantinople in a small chapel belonging to the Orthodox, while all the rest of the churches were taken over by Arians. From this small stronghold, called the Chapel of Anastasia, Gregory launched an attack against the heretics.[10]

When Theodosius was invited by Gratian in 379 to take up the coreign of the empire, he found a chaotic situation because of the inner divisions and fighting within Byzantium. According to Socrates, the church historian, the impact of religion was so strong on public affairs that the first of Theodosius's tasks was to bring about peace and to lead the churches to agreement. Being firmly Orthodox, he threw all of his energy into preventing the heretics from

[7]Basil of Caesarea, *Adversus Eunomium* 5, 2 (PG 29.753).
[8]Epiphanius, *Contra Haereses* 69 (PG 42.289).
[9]Gregory Nazianzus, *Epistola* 102 (PG 37.193).
[10]*Contra Arianos* (PG 36.257); Theodoret, *The Ecclesiastical History* 5, 9 (PG 82.1213).

disturbing the established faith and order. Moreover, Theodosius was aware of his responsibilities toward Western Christendom, particularly its two great leaders: Damasus, bishop of Rome, and Ambrose of Milan. Fortunately, in pursuing this difficult task, Theodosius was supported by the wisdom and advice of two outstanding bishops, Ascholius of Thessalonica and Meletius of Antioch.

Since it was the emperor who convoked the bishops in synod, one might conclude that such a Constantinopolitan intervention was inadmissible inasmuch as the secular arm could be seen interfering in church affairs. One must remember, however, that in the eyes of the free church, after a long period of persecution and shaken by heretics and schismatics, the emperor was acting in his capacity to represent the whole laity, the people of God. The custom was that the emperor assisted in all practical matters of the church, providing money and guards for the delegates on their long and often dangerous trips across the seas and through inhospitable regions. This practice was already established by Constantine the Great, who summoned the First Ecumenical Council of Nicaea. Consequently, Theodosius was following the same line, *"ex sacerdotum sententia . . . ,"* as the historian Rufinus stated.[11]

The Second Ecumenical Council of 381 consisted of one hundred fifty delegates gathered exclusively from the eastern region of the empire. It completed its work in a very short time (May and June) under the presidency of Meletius of Antioch (who died during that time), Gregory of Nazianzus, and his successor to the imperial see in Constantinople, Nectarius.

The objectives set by the Council were the following: to deal with the christological conflicts and the other corrosive factors introduced by Arianism; to refute the Pneumatomachians of Macedonius; to formulate concretely the Orthodox faith; to prescribe ecclesiastical order and discipline; to determine the boundaries of the jurisdiction of the local churches; and to fix the honorary place of the see of Constantinople through binding canons.

The Creed which emerged was a real enrichment, as Gregory of Nazianzus noted, "by correcting what was imperfectly said, since previously the matter had not been raised at all."[12] And this was done, as the fathers of the Ecumenical Council of Chalcedon speci-

---

[11]*Church History* 1, 217 (PG 21.467).
[12]*Epistola* 102 (PG 37.193).

fied, "not as introducing something missing from what was previously provided, but as demonstrating more clearly with scriptural witness its article concerning the Holy Spirit against those who attempted to diminish its domination."[13]

In fact, the most crucial problem was the trinitarian doctrine. The words of St. Athanasius became a dogmatic dictum for all times:

> Theology is perfect in the Trinity. This is the only true piety, and this is the truth and the good. It is the faith which the Lord himself gave, the apostles preached and the fathers kept. It is the faith on which the church is built. The trinitarian unity is seen in the trinitarian economy of salvation. In this trinitarian economy, the Three Persons act in unison. The Father saves, the Son saves, the Spirit saves. This unit is not based on the knowledge of God's being, but on the knowledge of the one saving act of the Triune God.[14]

The Nicene Creed is generally accepted as providing a summary of our Christian faith. It has been used by all, from the time of its origin, as the basis of the faith of the baptized; it is proclaimed by all of us during eucharistic assemblies. One may single out the components of this confession of faith as follows:

- Creeds and the Nicene Creed
- God—Creation—man's responsibilities
- Effects of Christ's incarnation
- Ecclesiology: one holy catholic and apostolic church

[13]Giovanni Domenico Mansi, *Sacrorum Conciliorum Nova et Amplissima Collectio* (31 vols., 1759–98) 7, 108.
[14]*Contra Arianos* I (PG 26.49); *Letter to Serapion* I (PG 26.596 and 605).

The Creed and Creeds

UNLIKE THE FRAMERS of ancient Greek theogonies and cosmogonies, early Christian apologists used another approach, since God is without origin and is eternal. Athenagoras the Athenian (second century) rejected mythology and polytheism in a neat theological statement: "We acknowledge also a Son of God. Let no one think it ridiculous that God should have a Son. For though the poets, in their fictions, represent the gods as no better than men, our mode of thinking is not the same as theirs, concerning either God the Father or the Son."[15] Justin succinctly stated his profession of faith as follows:

> When we say that the Logos, who is the firstborn of God, was produced without sexual union and that Jesus Christ, our Teacher, was crucified and died, and rose again and ascended into heaven, we propound nothing different from what you believe regarding the honorable sons of Jupiter! For you know how many sons your esteemed writers have ascribed to Jupiter, Mercury, Aesculapius, Bacchus, Hercules, Dioscuri, Perseus, and Bellerophon.[16]

The task of the fathers during the Second Ecumenical Council was to focus in very brief and strong terms on God's lordship, and to consider this matter not in human categories but as a corpus of truth revealed to us by the Holy Spirit.[17] True theological knowledge for the Cappadocians (Basil of Caesarea, Gregory of Nazianzus, and Gregory of Nyssa) has a catholic character, inasmuch as it is accessible to all people. As the gospel of salvation, it has a universal appeal. It extends to the "entire *oekumene* from end to end of the heavens. It includes all people and all ages, men, women, children, and the aged who especially find rest in this great gift."[18]

[15]*Embassy* 10 (PG 6.908).
[16]*Apology* I, 21 (PG 6.1360).
[17]See Basil of Caesarea's *Adversus Eunomium* (PG 29.601).
[18]Gregory of Nazianzus, *Oratio* 27, 3 (PG 36.13, 44.437, and 46.600b).

Patristics do not abolish human intelligence. Rather, they repudiate
the kind of degraded human subjectivism which treats God as an
object that can be known or determined by humans. "God is not an
object of curiosity but a free and sovereign being who gives himself
to be known by a created being, who is equally respected for its
own subjective integrity and expected to be willingly and freely
related to God. This faith has gathered together men from east,
west, north, and the sea into the knowledge of God."[19]

For the fathers, divine truth is not something expressed so
openly. God's truth often is silent, mysterious, invisible. Basil of
Caesarea says that the mysteries of the church are unwritten.[20] At
the same time, however, these secret truths are the explicitly dynamic, saving, living Word, according to the Pauline expression:
"the mystery hidden from the ages and generations but now made
manifest to his saints" (Col. 1:26). It seems that among the fathers
there persisted the view that this truth could be known only
through and within the church. Clement of Alexandria refers to the
"gnosis of God" incorporated in the tradition of the church in
secret, so as not to be profaned by the noninitiated.[21] Basil also
refers to truth as veiled in silence.[22]

That this tradition is silent is confirmed by Ignatius of Antioch
who, when speaking of the reality of the Word of God, says, "He
who possesses in truth the word of Jesus can hear even his silence."[23]
This privileged faculty echoes the very words of Christ, "He who
has ears to hear, let him hear" (Matt. 11:15). The truths of God
cannot be captured only by fleshly ears. This implies a conversion
of the heart, an awakening to the vertical dimension, so that revelation is understood not only in breadth but also in depth and height
(Eph. 3:18).

Here enters the double nature of the given tradition: the horizontal and the vertical. Philosophers since Plato and Aristotle have
accepted a whole world of "ideas" scattered in the universe which
can be attained by intellectual research, thus becoming enrichment

[19]Origen, *Commentary on the Proverbs* (PG 17.229).
[20]*De Spiritu Sancto* 27 (PG 32.188–192).
[21]*Stromateis* 6–61.
[22]*De Spiritu Sancto* 27 (PG 32.189).
[23]*Letter to the Ephesians* 15, 2.

for our earthly existence. Noble ideas concerning art, music, harmony, and technology are available, only they must be found and properly utilized. All of these concern the horizontal dimension.

In addition, there is the vertical "gnosis" of the otherworldly reality, that which is beyond human intellect. The Spirit of God works out his economy by inspiring, guiding, and illuminating those pure in heart in the church. Only in such an "ecclesial" way can one grasp this knowledge and experience so that from the periphery one can advance to the very core of truth. This wealth does not consist so much in detailed rules, rites, and observations, but in redeeming messages and communications, invisible and sanctifying, which lead people to their glorious goal. Similarly, one can say that the books of the Old Testament—written or compiled over many centuries, the work of various authors, and incorporating different religious traditions—possess only an accidental unity between them for a historian of religions. However, a true member of Christ's church will immediately recognize the Spirit at work, inspiring the same faith within this variety—the Spirit who spoke through the "mouth of the prophets" in the ancient alliance and who, when the fullness of time came, enabled the Mother of God to conceive the Logos in flesh. Thus one must be in the church to admire the unity as well as the variety of God's interventions in history, which together constitute the *oikonomia* of our salvation. Of course, a Christian in such cases must follow the advice of Origen who, before the multitude of unreliable religious traditions circulating and claiming authenticity, recommended a critical "attention," rejecting those in error. In so doing, he followed St. Paul's encouragement to "test everything" and "hold fast what is good" (1 Thess. 5:21).[24] Such a critical attitude was typical of Maximus the Confessor with regard to the Corpus Dionysiacum, a series of theological writings highly esteemed by the Monophysites and attributed to Dionysius the Areopagite. After subjecting them to close analysis, Maximus declared them to be an expression of the patristic rather than of the apostolic tradition.

Christian perception goes beyond any structuralism or epistemology as Aristotle understood it. We know Aristotle's aphorism:

[24]See Origen's *Commentary on Matthew* 28.

"There is nothing in the mind which was not first in the senses." In his *Metaphysics* and *Analytics*, Aristotle expressly states that sense perception is the foundation of his entire theory of knowledge. In seeking to explain how higher knowledge develops out of more primitive forms, he traces all forms of knowledge, animal and human, to a common source, "an innate critical faculty which is called sense perception." Aristotle does not suggest that this is the end of the epistemological road. His scheme includes language, rational knowledge, creative intellect, and even, alas, metaphysics; but he unequivocally states that this is where knowledge begins and where we must begin if we are to understand his metaphysics. The trouble with structuralism, like all forms of idealism, is that it takes the mind for granted and fails to inquire into its aptitudes. In *De Anima* he states that "no one could ever learn or understand anything except by way of sense perception."[25] Aristotle once suggested that the skeptic should take a brisk walk to the edge of a precipice: if he stopped at the edge, that would be the end of skepticism; if he did not, that would be the end of the skeptic. This gives some insight into the importance Aristotle attached to sense perception.

A few words are in order with regard to the physiognomy of these ancient creeds in general, and of the Constantinopolitan in particular. They are not at all similar to posterior "symbolic books" issued in the West in order to show their close similarity to the faith of the ancient church and consequently their credibility. Neither the *Confessio Augustana* nor any other such creedal text of Rome or the Reformation under whatever name can be compared. These creeds are rather detailed texts of a particular confessional family— casuistic, accidental, incomplete, and missing, therefore, the authority of catholicity, a general consensus. They are literally "confessional," reflecting particular problems of bodies for the sake of their own preservation. They are contextual too, since they seek to answer specific questions.

It is certain that the undivided early church avoided judging current beliefs in detail. An ecumenical council did not assess political or social situations, nor discuss pagan views or philosophical doctrines. It rejected errors, but a council considered it sufficient to

[25]*De Anima* 432a.

project its faith in general, without scrupulous analysis. Numerous errors of our time, seemingly new, are in reality the rebirth of old heresies under new names. The tendency to define everything exactly and to find for each problem a right or wrong theological solution violates the principle of theological liberty, confusing unity with uniformity. It was felt that a great area of freedom should be left for the "theologoumena" or "adiaphora." As Gregory of Nazianzus says:

> Philosophize about the universe, or the universes . . . about the resurrection, the judgment, the retribution, the sufferings of Christ, for in these subjects it is not without usefulness to press on to the end, especially since it is not dangerous to be in error. But let us pray to God for success, in a small degree now, and later, perhaps, in a more perfect way in Jesus Christ himself.[26]

In other words, on questions of creation, redemption, and everything else concerning the future and the present life, Christians are free to meditate according to their piety. "This is not dangerous," Gregory says. The church does not want to scrutinize, to dictate, to impose, and to formulate in the smallest detail all questions in a conciliar way. Orthodox faith is neither an impediment nor a fetter to thought. It is no more than preserving definitions by means of which the church wants to place human reason in the necessary perspective for opening to it the possibility of an unencumbered and unhalting progression, avoiding the dangers of a deviation into deceiving ways. No conciliar creed repeated what had already been said, nor was it a mosaic of texts and patristic quotations, but a reliable direction and guide offering freedom for thinking and formulating or applying a truth to given situations and cases.

In the mind of the fathers was the firm conviction of the need for a written *formula unionis* acceptable to all, certainly with the understanding of a reliable statement of faith which would assure, on the one hand, the faithful orthodox of their legitimate membership in the one church and, on the other, lead all those heretics driven away for one or another reason to see their errors and return to their mother church. Such a creedal statement was intended to be a means of strengthening the fellowship-*koinonia* of the churches of Christ scattered throughout the empire and elsewhere. Due to

[26]*Homily* 28.

the gravity of the situation, it was the only way to bring back and facilitate the reintegration of schismatic groups. In fact, it became the exclusive, synoptic basis of the fullness of the Orthodox faith. Without intending to supplant Holy Scripture or the other ancient postapostolic creedal texts, it simply aimed to make the proclamation of the faith more actual and stronger in dynamic terms, corresponding to the needs of that time.

Strangely enough, up to that time the Nicene Creed still remained a text for limited and rare occasions. It was a Monophysite bishop, famous for his liturgical knowledge, Peter the Fuller (d. 488), who first incorporated it into the Liturgy. In order to show his "orthodoxy" to his Orthodox adversaries, he took the initiative of incorporating it into public eucharistic worship. During the sixth century this status of being part of the Liturgy for the first time in the church of Antioch gradually gave the Creed a universal authority. It was not only its catholic reception that gave it such status or prestige but also the instrument which formulated it—the catholic conciliar body of reliable representatives of the churches offered it a unique, incontestable authenticity.

In the ancient church, the custom prevailed that when a heresy appeared, it was the task of the local church, before anybody else, to face and combat it. The next step was that this particular church informed the other churches of this happening, making known in the spirit of *koinonia* the danger to the common Orthodox faith. This was done through canonical encyclical letters. Thus a particular action was made known to the others and confirmed by the *pleroma* of the whole body of Christ. Each separate church thus expressed the self-consciousness of the whole church. So as long as this local church maintained the bond with the Holy Spirit, it was not necessary to have an additional support—a horizontal confirmation. Each church itself was understood to constitute a synod.

In a similar fashion, during its deliberations, a council does not produce new dogmas; it does not innovate. Rather, it simply reinterprets and reformulates what exists in substance in the catholic faith or relates its value to new emerging situations in the continuous life and daily realities of the church. The church has the right to distinguish the truth from the deviations held by heretics. In doing this, each church tests whether a particular teaching stands within the true faith or not, whether it is in continuity with the apostles' faith. This explains why in such conciliar texts we often meet the expressions: "following," "in accordance," "in conformity," and "faithful to the symphonia."

There is no doubt that the implications of all the creeds were not always easily understood by all. One of the many other reasons put forward for the breakdown of ecclesiastical unity in the early church is the difficulty in translating theological realities into corresponding terms. The West had great difficulty in seizing the implications of the dogmatic terminology in the original Greek and rendering it into Latin. As a language, Latin was not so rich as to be able to render the corresponding terms exactly. Gregory of Nazianzus sincerely admits the hidden perils of translation and warns church leaders not to fall into the trap of semantics, which is a phenomenological problem. In fact, both theologians of East and West were wrestling to find a language capable of expressing the mysteries of our faith. Once this was done in Greek, Western theologians were unable to formulate it into their respective words. Often the translation was approximate. Gregory makes a plea on the grounds of "verbal poverty" and ambiguities in semantics not to transfer linguistic quarrels and differences into the field of the faith. Such real dangers for St. Gregory were emerging from the terms: *ousia, hypostasis, physis theotētos, idiōtēs, prosōpon.* Sabellianism and Arianism were already exploiting such small linguistic differences.[27]

The irreducible difficulties of any dialogue stem from this monadic condition of linguistics. Each lives in other space. We lodge within a "time-space," which determines the forces at work in a given culture, and the horizons and perspectives of perception and recognition. Thus, it gives to every word its singular historicity, determining the possible resonances and oscillations of meaning within certain bounds of time and space. There exist in fact immense worlds within words. The *heteroglossia* entails that the interpreter of a text, who inevitably operates under conditions other than those of the original enunciation, cannot without difficulty fully capture and analyze the primal core, the meaning of meaning, in any semantic moment. Every written text is part of an ambient whole.

The confession of the faith as contained in the Nicene Creed

[27]Gregory of Nazianzus, *Sermon* 32, 3; see also *Sermon* 21, 35.

should be taken as an undivided whole. It is a concise exposition of the common faith of the universal church. Its articles are interrelated, interdependent, and complementary. Nobody has the right to isolate one article from the rest. Their coherence is seen in the organic order in which they are listed by the inspired fathers: God loves his creatures; God sends his Son for our salvation; the Holy Spirit has its own place in the history of salvation, being the Lord, the life-giver and, therefore, worshipped together with the other persons of the Holy Trinity. It is also of high importance to put the emphasis upon the attributes of the church. These attributes or marks constitute the distinctive traits, the *notae ecclesiae,* of the true *ecclesia* from other, heretical bodies.

Now comes a series of paradoxes and contradictions while we celebrate the sixteen hundredth anniversary of the Creed. In those days this Creed could not be read by a schismatic or heretic intent upon denying its contents and fighting the church. Reading the Creed was the exclusive privilege of those holding the "orthodox" faith. Since the days when the Creed was first composed, we have had to face many strange, incomprehensible attitudes. The great separation took place in 1054 between Rome and Constantinople, and yet the same text of the Creed is maintained by these two divided major bodies, except for the *Filioque* clause interpolated by the West. In the sixteenth century when the Reformation occurred with all its sad consequences, nobody intended to reject this Creed. What nevertheless happened is a different reading of the text by theologians; each one gives a different meaning to it. Each one refers to the ancient church as if it belongs to him, each invoking separately the apostolic and postapostolic teaching. Unity is broken. The Eucharist is no longer administered reciprocally, although the intercommunion issue or *communicatio in sacris* has in recent years come up again and again.

Let us remember the increasing number of further misinterpretations and deviations. Instead of confessing one God, Father almighty, a theology of "God is dead" has appeared, claiming God's defeat before other forces and his failure in world history. Radical, unorthodox theories on Jesus' humanity, attaching more importance to it than to his divinity, are widespread, thus portraying Jesus as an opponent of the ruling class, misusing the Pauline view of kenotic Christology or the servant idea of Deutero-Isaiah—a great

revolutionary humanist or a Savior Christ. The Holy Spirit is often
identified with a vague esoteric tranquillity and not presented as a
distinctive person of the Holy Trinity. Others have objectivized the
Spirit, viewing the Spirit as a certain amount of grace and forgetting
that the Spirit is not object but subject—*prosōpon,* God.

Particularities of
Creedal Texts

ONCE AND FOR ALL it must be said that most of the terms used in the Nicene Creed are taken from the New Testament and some from patristic quotations. Already the fathers, in fighting Arians and Eunomians, had established a unique and standard language. Such formulas became current expressions, summarizing the content of the Orthodox faith. There are considerable terms and expressions which, therefore, cannot be properly understood outside of their ecclesiastical or liturgical context. We have to see them with the same eyes, to test and understand them with the same spirit (the *consensus ecclesiae*), and to live them as they were lived within the sacramental life of the church. There is a continuity and inter-dependence between the proclamation of faith and the religious life of a baptized Christian.

Here we acknowledge an extraordinary phenomenon, namely, that while many things have since changed, the faith of the church remains the same. Sustained by the same Holy Spirit, the church receives the same guidance, has the same mystical experience, and lives the same realities as in the early centuries. What St. Paul, Athanasius of Alexandria, John Chrysostom, and others proclaimed in those days is valid today and even tomorrow. This is why whenever a conciliar or patristic term appears in whatever language, we must see what the church throughout the ages understands by these words. Such texts often appear simple but in fact require much meditation. Doctrinal truths express a deep spiritual message and can only be grasped by devotional effort. Through them the Spirit breaks down the obstacles and speaks and communicates saving truths. Humility and *kenosis* are needed in studying the Creed.

In the Apophthegmata Patrum an interesting story is recorded about Paul the Simple, an Egyptian ascetic. One day, after listening to Anthony the Great read the first verse of the Psalm, "Oh, the joys of the man who walks not after the advice of the wicked, nor stands in the path of sinners, nor sits in the seat of scoffers," he fled into the desert. Only after thirty years did they both meet each other again, and Paul said to Anthony, in deep humility: "I have spent the whole time since in order to become that type of man who walks not after the advice of the wicked!"

Clement of Alexandria warns those who wish to penetrate into doctrinal texts of the amount of hardships involved and the need for a living faith:

> The readiness acquired by previous training conduces much to the perception of such things as are requisite; but those things which can be perceived by mind only are the special exercise of the mind. And their nature is triple according as we consider their quantity, their magnitude, and what can be predicated of them.

> For the discourse which consists of demonstrations implants clear faith in the spirit of him who follows it; so that he cannot conceive of that which is demonstrated being different. And so it does not allow us to succumb to those who assail us by fraud. In such studies, therefore, the soul is purged from sensible things and is excited so as to be able to see truth distinctly. For nutriment and the training which is maintained gentle make noble natures; and noble natures, when they have received such training, become still better than before both in other respects, but especially in productiveness, as is the case with the other creatures. Therefore, it is said: "Go to the ant, thou sluggard, and become wiser than it, which provides much and varied food in the harvest against the inclemency of winter" (Prov. 6:6, 8).[28]

To become familiar with such conciliar language is not easy. It requires special attention. Thus during the eucharistic Liturgy, we are often reminded: "Let us attend," and let us "take heed." This is said before the reading of a scriptural pericope; special perception is necessary, since God himself is to speak at that very moment.

For the history of our divisions, it is useful to remember that the Nicene Creed is recognized by many confessional families and is even used in their worship services. A difficulty arises when an article of the Creed is taken separately in support of a particular theological thesis. It is this which creates a frustration and uneasiness among the many churches that issued from the Reformation which, although they constantly make use of ancient creeds, do not have corresponding ecclesiastical structures or a sense of con-

[28]*Stromateis,* I, vi, 35, 2–5 (PG 8.728–29).

tinuity. Of course, everyone is free to refer to ancient sources for their credibility. But confirmation of such credibility, *bebaiosis*, by the visible facts, is quite a different matter. Inconsistency and anomaly occur in many theological positions and compel an objective reader to be cautious in view of texts that claim apostolic faithfulness.

The attitude of the church has rightly been the maintenance of the wholeness of truth, since unity is indivisible and thus capable of unbroken continuity. Hence the faith formulated in the Creed of the First Ecumenical Council of 325 appears in the Creed of the Second Council of 381. This remarkable convergence was the responsibility of the episcopacy which, from the time of Ignatius of Antioch, had entrusted to it the mandate *parakatathēkē*, to watch with vigilance over the maintenance of truth.

In fact, many early documents emphasized that the particular *diaconia* of episcopacy was to be the guarantee of ecclesiastical unity and the purity of the faith by defending its integrity against heretics, schismatics, or any falsificators—and, consequently, to be the true *didaskalos*, distinguishing the error, the *pseudodidaskalia* or heterodoxy. It is in this context that one must understand the occasional sharp interventions coming after a reserved attitude, as the episcopacy became aware of the dangers to the faith entrusted to them and took antiheretical action. This action was in different forms, one of them being the synodical system of conciliarity.

According to the importance of the dangers, councils took on different arithmetic size, often including local clergy and invited neighboring clergy from other local churches. Such corporate action was dictated by recognition that each had common defense duties and that faith constituted a common gift. The community of action was intimately related to the common ordinations of bishops by bishops from other churches, and the exchange of letters on urgent problems and on other matters. Sister churches could not be ignored since together they all constituted the one and same body of Christ. Thus was assured the consensus of the oneness, and the solemn affirmation of unanimity found its corporate expression in eucharistic concelebration and communion. Anyone differing in doctrine or being in schism was excluded from the same chalice. This is why today the pressing appeals for intercommunion meet with skeptical reluctance. As long as the doctrinal obstacles remain, this *communicatio in sacris* remains inoperative. The very mystery of the church is manifested in its *mysteria*. In other words, Eucharist is not an autonomous sacrament of love-agape only; it is, at the same time, the sacrament par excellence of unity. Therefore, we cannot use two different criteria, one from A.D. 381 and another now. What was valid and workable for discerning the truth against departures from the truth and errors in those days is applicable now too in order to discern which body is authentic, bearing the two distinctive marks of the church, and which is not.

God as Creator and Man as Steward of the Creation

THE FIRST ARTICLE of the Nicene Creed deals with the creative action of God and his continuous after-care. This leads us to an inquiry into the purpose, the "why" of both—the universe and man while on earth. Unless we find the *telos* or purpose of the created world, we are in danger of taking the universe in a static way, as a continuous reservoir which provides raw material for our avidity, selfishness, and unlimited consumption. Yet this confession of faith in God as Creator, from the most ancient time of Israel, was not a subject for scientific curiosity regarding how and when the world came to be, based on economic or productive processes. Rather, it incited man to investigate the reason for creation, the place of man in this universe, and how to express his feelings about God: admiration and responsibility as well.

Admiration for the whole cosmos is included in man's stewardship of the creation. For Origen, cosmos meant the richest ornament beautifying the creation. Cosmos is identical to beauty; thus cosmetics. The creation is given to man with all of its mysteries, order, harmony, immensity, and beauty—but also with its tragic side. Man is not only an explorer, a consumer of its richness, and a spectator, walking, enjoying, and doing nothing else. In fact, man must see the whole of nature as a gift, a mandate, a stewardship for which he has a grave responsibility. He must not restrict his relationship with the natural world to conquering its natural resources beyond measure until he destroys the world, at the same time destroying himself. His task lies, rather, in looking at the universe as an enormous field for contemplation, a means of gratitude and doxological praise.

For his investigation, modern man must bear in mind the crisis of the fifth and sixth centuries in the history of Israel, when the great Temple in Jerusalem was destroyed and the Jews were exiled to Babylon. In this crisis Israel was questioning faith in Yahweh as savior, as a faithful protector from heathen neighbors in crucial moments. The same doubt was expressed by Deutero-Isaiah, the author of the Book of Job, and the author of the first chapter of Genesis. According to the Genesis account, an orderly world is offered to man in order to worship the Maker of heaven and earth. Isaiah 40 interprets the creation as a kind of first liberation from chaos and death. He reminds an exhausted people in exile that creation and redemption are two closely interrelated terms. The same God, who for the pleasure of man had created the universe, will liberate his own chosen people from Babylon as they had been liberated at another time from Egypt. The author of the Book of Job is confronted with suffering and evil which in moments of despair seem to deny goodness and the sovereignty of God over humanity and history. Thus Job is invited to change his outlook, to meditate on the beauty of the world instead of on his sufferings; not to condemn himself to a forced silence, but to see the light hidden in the clouds: the presence and the love of God. Creation and poetry go together. Man thus learns that he is not the measure and center of all but a witness proclaiming God's wonders and his epiphanies, conscious of a strong love and affection which embraces and sustains him throughout his struggles. To dispel the pessimism among so many Christians, we need a new understanding of the sovereignty of God Pantocrator for whose purposes all history is inexorably being worked out.

In his *Praeparatio evangelica*, Eusebius of Caesarea (263–339) emphasizes the two poles around which Hebrew theology moves, namely, the doctrine of God the Creator and the doctrine of God the Supreme Actor in history, who provides and saves:

> Such is the theology of the Hebrews, which first teaches that all things were constituted by a creative word of God, and then goes on to teach that the entire universe was not left abandoned as an orphan deprived of a father by the one who constituted it, but that it is governed by the providence of God unto eternity, since God is not only creator and maker of all, but also savior, governor, king and chieftain, watching over sun and moon and stars and the entire heaven and world throughout the ages, and viewing all as through a great eye and divinely inherent power, and ordering and governing all things in the world.[29]

[29]Eusebius, *Praeparatio evangelica* II, 4 (PG 21.537).

The Nicene Creed passes from the creation to Christ's incarnation in order to show the depth and the immense love of God for human beings. He was incarnate for us, for our salvation. Here we have the height of divine *synkatabasis*. This condescendence of Christ aims to restore the fallen humanity. This action is linked to the institution of the church which exists in order to continue Christ's redeeming action, to bring human beings to the blessings of the Holy Trinity, and to create a *koinonia*. Here lies the mystery of the church's mission on earth. Thus Christology is linked with ecclesiology and soteriology. The fathers, anticipating deviations, treated Christ-church, head-body, together. St. Augustine said, *"Christus totus."*

Orthodox theology, exploring the mystery of God's care for mankind, explains that by God's very nature he is active, not withdrawn from the scene of history or immobile in a corner. Thus, in the Bible we find so many indications—surely anthropomorphic—of his continuous care and love, indications that God exists, God sees, God listens, God intervenes. God loves, speaks to us, sends, asks our collaboration, judges, rewards, punishes, and saves (or rather, God is saving continuously). The problem that emerges is the following: How does God act and manifest himself in all of these movements? How do we understand his saving activities? For instance, when we say that God exists, we must recognize that he does not exist in the same way that we exist as human beings. We are created and finite, but he is uncreated and infinite. God sees certainly, but unlike the limited possibilities of men. His field of action and vision has no limits. God loves, but with an immeasurable, infinite love. There are indeed limits for us as finite human beings in our ability to understand how God is behaving here and now. Because of our limitations and our inability to understand, we use the apophantic way of understanding God and his actions, when we want to raise our research to godly issues. Patristics understands God's ways not through the philosophical methods of Plato, Aristotle, or even Plotinus, but through the Gospels: the *via affirmationis, via negationis, et via eminentiae.*

All begins, in fact, with an affirmation: God is, sees, loves, judges. He continues his relationship with the creation, but with a negation: God is not like me. God does not see like me. God does not love like me. God does not judge like me. Real theology is *docta ignorantia*. This *agnosia*, this "not-knowing" of human nature, is expressed by negative formulas which are even then poor and inadequate. Instead of saying that God sees, we prefer to say that God does not ignore. It is, therefore, necessary if we want to understand the relationship between God and man in the work of salvation to follow the three successive ways which constitute the unique means of reaching transcendent truth. Thus, when we say that God does all, that he is the unique author of our salvation, we must understand that it is not a kind of ready-made salvation. He makes and takes all appropriate steps so that we might also work out our salvation and do this entirely free from any constraint or force. As Ezekiel has said: "I will put my spirit within you, and cause you to walk in my statutes and be careful to observe my ordinances" (Ezek. 36:27). St. Augustine insists on such a twofold action, implying a continuous initiative, response, and cooperation between God's first cause on one side and man's answer on the other: *"facium ut faciatis,"* that is, "I shall be doing and then you will be doing."

"It is certain that when we will, in fact it is we who will, but it is he, the God, who makes that we might want the good . . . It is certain that when we do, it is we that do, but it is he who enables us to do it."[30]

In this respect, there are the words of Christ: "Apart from me you can do nothing" (John 15:5). It becomes evident that this cooperation does not confine itself purely to abstract or sentimental matters, to contemplation and prayer alone. Cooperation leads on to our sharing with God, thus creating a kind of co-redemption. In cosmic dimensions, the divine plan seeks our redemption—the *opus redemptionis nostrae*. Our real cooperation depends on the degree of our acceptance or rejection of the *offered* (but otherwise mysterious) collaboration of man with God, with all of its possibilities in the field of our salvation. Through his incarnation, Christ makes us partakers of his divinity. He enables us to fulfill all of our responsibilities. If, due to the law of human solidarity, the first Adam made us sinners by his rebellion, the second Adam—that is, Christ—on the contrary constitutes us saints in him and by him. We become members of Christ. All good proceeds from him, the head of his body.

[30]Augustine, *Of Grace and Free Will*, c32.

Our Ascending Process

GOD'S TRANSCENDENCE is essential to theology. The efforts of process theologians to narrow the gulf are often impressive, but they are destined to fall short. For instance, if it is a matter of what the future will bring, then all we are saying is that God has a higher batting average than we humans do in our attempts at prediction. If we try to save God's omnipotence by redefining it as present power or constancy of character but limit him in other ways, such as in his ability to command nature, then we are plainly not talking about omnipotence. If we try to reconcile his sovereignty with his limitations by ascribing the latter to a divine voluntary renunciation of power, then we are not talking about real limits, but expressing our beliefs about God's nature as love. If we claim to have made the presence of natural evil compatible with a good and wise God by blaming it on nature's freedom of choice among possibilities and on man's reaction to natural events, we are still left wondering why God chose to allow evil possibilities. We may try to restore the idea of divine transcendence by appealing to appropriate metaphors, suggesting that God transcends the world as a man does his body. But as long as the world truly limits God's possibilities, no metaphor can recover the kind of transcendence known to biblical spirituality.

Love and suffering flow from God and do not really limit him. Transcendence is better seen as a more serviceable concept than the kind of immanence which restricts God against his will. It is quite enough to say that the world affects God but not that he truly depends on it for his own existence.

Theōsis—*Deification*

THE HEART OF New Testament anthropology lies in the belief that man does not live for himself or exclusively for this earthly life. Nor is it he who determines his ultimate goal. Any anthropocentric conception of man is refuted by the assertion of a radically christocentric anthropology. Man is then created in order that he may put himself and all his gifts at the service of God and shape his daily life according to the divine will. Only if he fulfills these conditions can he become completely and authentically man. But if he does obey these conditions, if he does "live in Christ," then he can hope to attain this full and authentic manhood precisely because Christ, being God, first assumed full human nature. In so doing, Christ restored to human nature its original virtue, which had been lost after the fall, and endowed man with such spiritual powers that, although he still belongs to the fallen world, he is enabled to achieve salvation and to become "like unto God." St. Clement of Alexandria speaks of this elevation of human nature in remarkable terms in his *Paedagogus*:

> I maintain that God has created man from earth, regenerated him through water, arranged for his spiritual growth—educating him through the word, guiding him toward sonship and salvation by the divine commandments; and all this in order to re-create man the transgressor as a saintly and heavenly being, so that the divine utterance "Let us create man according to the image and likeness of God" (Gen. 1:26) might be fulfilled. Christ accomplished this to the full according to God's words.[31]

The practical consequence of this elevation of human nature is that man is protected from falling into moral and spiritual disorder. He is protected from falling into narcissism and self-admiration. The Narcissus of Greek mythology, or no matter what period of

---

[31]Clement, *Paedagogus* 1, 12.

history he may live in, never admits the validity of anything beyond himself. He deifies self-sufficiency and frequently looks at himself in his mirror. He is dangerously subjective and overestimates himself. Otherwise he might fall victim to despair and nihilism. Both of these excesses stem from the fact that he does not look in the mirror of God's Word, that is, Christ and his Word, and consequently creates erroneous pictures of himself and his neighbors.

Thus a major question arises: what is man's relation to the natural order? Fundamentally, this is a theological question. Not only contemporary theologians, but even the fathers have investigated the relevance of faith to the problem of man in his environment. For the last few centuries, Western theology has become increasingly man-centered. As all notions of purpose, meaning, and value have been expelled from the scientific view of the cosmos, they have had to be sought within man himself. Theology has withdrawn from the external Word to confine itself to a dangerously narrow field of pietism with an exclusively "spiritual" dimension. In consequence, man and his world have fallen apart. The consequences of this myopic approach have been disastrous.

Man protests henceforth that he is alienated both from the world and from his fellowmen, and he tends to behave aggressively toward both. For in this view, nature is merely a thing, without value or meaning in its own right, to which we owe no moral obligation; it is just raw material to be exploited.

Can one postulate a religious, well-balanced world view involving a common order for man and his work and for organic and inorganic nature—all related to one another? Liturgical theology could provide a reasonable framework, for it warns against limiting its scope to man's subjectivity. Either it must speak, however tentatively, about God as Creator and all that entails, or it speaks adequately about nothing, not even about man in his subjectivity. For man, who transcends nature, is part of nature. We are, therefore, invited to reassess, to reconsider the traditional doctrine of creation. The strength of such a treatment will lie in its full acceptance of the most recent scientific discoveries but without divinizing DNA.

"God created heaven and earth," that is to say, all things that exist. The word used for "created" denotes activity in a unique mode, what God can do but no other being can. The world is not

God—not numinous or adorable. From the first verse of Genesis, it is desacralized. But it depends upon God for its existence, restoration, orderly functioning, and continuous care—*oikonomia*—and, therefore, should be approached with reverence. As for man, he is set apart from nature. He is given privileged dominion over the other creatures. Man's unique status in the cosmos, as *coadministrator*, is attested by the incarnation. Yet he is not the absolute, self-reliant, lord (*kyrios*) of the natural order, for such a role belongs to God alone.

Dominion over natural resources and physical potentialities has often been taken as suggesting human exploitation and blind imperialism over nature at their most blatant. Biblical and patristic teachings remind us that this human "dominion" is better understood in terms of a responsible stewardship, committed to man as *imago Dei*—the image of the God to whom man is answerable for its exercise. The world was not tailored to receive the entry of a passive and idle humanity. Man has had to be vigilant, to share in the maintenance and orderly running of the world—in Eden or out of it—thus becoming a partner of God through *synergeia*. Once man appeared on the scene, a new factor emerged which man henceforth was able to modify and, within his limits as a creature, to control.

It is God's plan that man will cooperate for the restoration of the fallen nature. Man should know that since the first disobedience, a multifaceted disorder (*ataxia*) entered history. The order established by God was not only broken, but its consequences touched the human race as well as the natural world. History since then has been influenced by this anomaly. Wars, genocide, injustice, exploitation, hate, and enmity have been introduced to such an extent that life has become a real drama. How then can *taxis* instead of *ataxia* change history and the cosmos? How can so many accumulated evils be removed and God's will prevail? In establishing a new order in the world, every human being has a role to play. All saintly people and especially ascetics, while praying, have been aiming at the restoration of the cosmos. If there is a universal meaning, the entire world must be reconciled.

Man is not an isolated being but is intimately connected with and inseparable from the other creatures. By his very nature, he is connected with the entire world. This cosmic awareness has always been inherent in patristic thought. On his path toward communion with God, man does not cast aside the creatures; instead, he shares the needs of all as if they were his own needs. In the ancient world, the idea of a moral responsibility for the creation was not so evident, because the idea of a creature with freedom did not exist. Christians look for redemption of the creation and its renewal; they agonizingly feel a sense of responsibility for it and for the conquest of evil. Many fathers have maintained that evil is nonexistent: "Nothing is evil by nature, but an evil thing becomes evil from the manner in which it is used," Methodius of Olympus used to say.[32] Such an understanding of evil compels us not to shut ourselves out from the world but to save the world itself. How can we cut ourselves off from the rest of the world when God shows the ocean of his love? Christ's incarnation has not only created the possibility of salvation but also faith in the *perfection* or *theōsis* of human nature. The concept of deification is most clearly expressed by Athanasius of Alexandria: "God became man in order that man might become godlike."[33]

Man's responsibility to creation stems from the relationship of God-world and Creator-creation, fixing man's place in the universe. The record of Genesis, in which Adam gives names to the animals, bears a profound significance, since a name is not here a mere sound but the vehicle of the substance. Man gives names to the creatures and so he becomes administrator, partner, *oikonomos*. In our time when the overexploitation of natural resources and the violation of biological equilibria create so much harm to the environment, causing pollution, danger to nature and to humankind, we have to change our approach to these gifts of God. Order can come about only by immensely "loving" as God loves, as Isaac the Syrian has said:

> A loving heart is a heart burning for all creation: for men, birds, animals, demons, all creatures . . . One who possesses this heart prays every hour with tears for the dumb creatures and for the enemies of truth, and for those who do him harm, so that they may be made pure and preserved; he also prays for every thing that

[32]*De libero arbitrio* (PG 18.264).
[33]*Oratio de incarnatione Verbi* 54 (PG 25.192).

creepeth, and great pity is stirred within his heart without measure after the likeness of God.[34]

Following these lines of the great ascetic, many saintly men and women of prayer have lived with wild animals peacefully as at the time of Adam, fully understanding the place of creation as a precious mandate to us. Man, being the crown and the head of the creation, is held responsible before God for the good functioning of the creation. Selfishness prevents us from seeing the world as a mandate. Sin disturbs this given commission so that we behave foolishly, disregarding effects for next generations as everything around us can be used or exploited as we like. Abuse of this responsibility consists in distorting the order. Such being the case, we are invited not to save ourselves from the world but to save the world itself, showing during this operation that the world belongs to the Lord of heaven and earth and, therefore, is not self-existing.

The fact that nobody can stay indifferent before nature, but each has to assume certain responsibilities, stems from man's very nature. Divine breath was diffused in him. Man was given an honorary task by the Holy Spirit, a partnership in *synergeia,* what Gregory of Nazianzus calls a "stream of Divinity, a particle of Divinity" and "even created as God."[35] Maximus the Confessor was to say: "Man by the grace of God can become that which God is in essence."[36] In other words, ontologically man is destined to become a partner in the divine plan for promoting the whole of creation into the ideal kingdom of God. Any static attitude, any resignation from such a mission is a betrayal or degradation. We cannot remain on earth as spectators, as mere consumers, casting a cynical eye on daily events and history and doing nothing. The two expressions of Genesis concerning man's substance, *imago Dei* and "likeness," give the key to his high potentialities. Gregory of Nyssa solemnly remarks: "The Creator approaches the making of man with due consideration, so as to prepare the substance for his composition and to liken his image to a certain prototypal beauty, and to designate the goal for which we exist."[37] The capacity for inner perfection

[34]*De Contemptu Mundi* (PG 86.411).
[35]*Poemata Mozalia,* sectio 2 (PG 37.685).
[36]*Centuria* III, 22 (PG 90.1024).
[37]*De hominis opificio* 3 (PG 44.133–36).

and improvement of the outside world lies in a dynamic striving toward God, his prototype. Macarius of Egypt asserts that only God and man are really free:

> You have been created in God's image and likeness, because God is his own master and does what he wishes. If he so desires, he can cast by virtue of his power the righteous into hell and take sinners into his kingdom. But the Lord does not approve of this and does not elect to do so, for he is just. So too are you your own master, but unstable in your nature, and, therefore, if you wish, you can perish, you can blaspheme, you can poison and kill and no one will stop you. However, on the other hand, if somebody wants to, he can submit himself to God, embark upon the road of righteousness, and be the master of his lusts.[38]

At all levels of existence, man can develop his genius and put even negative forces to work for the common good. This idea is expressed by Gregory Palamas:

> Out of all the creatures we alone possess, besides the sensory, also the nature of reason and logic. And the sensory, combined with the Logos, creates the variety of arts and sciences and comprehensions; it also creates the ability to till fields, build homes, and in general create from the nonexistent (although not from nothing altogether, for God alone can do this). And all of this is granted solely to people. Although nothing of what has been created by God is destroyed or isolated, but being juxtaposed one with the other, it obtains another form through us. And not only does the unseen word or the mind subordinate to itself the movement of the air and become a sensation of hearing, but it can also be written and can be seen in the body and through the body. God has given all of this to people alone, implementing for faith the advent in body and the appearance of the divine Logos. There has never been anything like this among the angels.[39]

Here one can see the dynamism of the ascending painful process of the "likeness to God." If God is the Creator, so also is man the "poet," king, priest, prophet, cobuilder, as St. Paul says, seeking the more perfect born for the better, dissatisfied with temporal and sensual pleasures, transforming the lower elements, elevating them, using negative powers in nature as energy for the advance of technology and the quality of life. The ascetic fathers described this upward process as *philocalia,* seeking the real beauty. Today as

[38]*Homily* 15, 23 (PG 34.591).
[39]*Capita physica,* theolog 620 (PG 150.1164–65).

yesterday, man's task is to respond to the creative word: "Let there be . . ." God awaits this from us. Humanity expects this from us. Man is responsible precisely because, being capable of speech and reason, he must multiply whatever gifts he has received with the whole of his being, with the plenitude of his humanity. This mystery of human creativity can be manifested in different spheres: spiritual, moral, social, economic, ecological, artistic, nuclear, scientific. How often one hears that faith is a personal affair and has nothing to do with the rest—that a Christian must seek his own salvation and ignore all of the rest.

The immense love of God for the world in revolt constitutes the permanent rule for action. This world needs a change, and the Christian's role is of paramount importance in bringing about change. The Christian has the privileged mission to preserve spiritual health and to fight the many forms of pollution—to be a peacemaker by reacting in a constructive way to injustice, hate, and a demoniac spirit. Consequently, an introvert and self-centered attitude becomes untenable. St. John Chrysostom has written the most challenging and critical pages against "private salvation":

> Let us not settle for the search for our own salvation; this would mean ruining it. If in a battle formation a soldier thinks only of how to save himself by escape, he destroys himself and his comrades in arms. A valiant soldier who fights for others saves himself alongside the others. Since our life is a war, the most cruel of wars, a battle, a fight in formation, let us remain in the ranks, as the king has commanded us to, prepared to strike, kill and shed blood [here he is referring, of course, to the spiritual warfare, the battle against sin], thinking about common salvation, spurring on those who are still on their feet, raising those lying on the ground. In this battle many of our brethren have fallen, been wounded, have spilt their blood, and no one shows concern for them, neither layman nor priest, none of their comrades in arms, friends, and brothers; each of us only pursues his own interests.[40]

Hence a sense of responsibility for nature and for man is incumbent upon us in all of our relations. A theological approach to this responsibility compels us to see the dimensions and the urgent need for a common action on the problems facing all of us.

"We believe in one God, the Father, the Almighty, maker of heaven and earth." Why did the fathers of the Council formulate

[40]Chrysostom (PG 58.509).

this first article? Above all, what is its relevance to the present religious crisis, people seeing God less and less as a Father or as omnipotent, and more and more as absent and silent in history?

At the outset we must make it clear that God's plan for salvation in history takes different shapes at different stages and moments, the climax being the redemptive action of Christ's incarnation and its continuity in this mystical body, the community of believers. After the creation, the "second creation," the incarnation of the Logos, becomes the very center of the whole of God's economy. Economy entails the *kenosis*, the most awesome mystery of Christ—his birth, the cross, the descent into hell, the resurrection, the ascension into heaven, and the glorious Second Coming, the Parousia. Of course, the economy of Christology cannot be separated from the economy in his church, that is, ecclesiology, the mystery of the church. "Mystery" here does not imply something totally obscure but rather something that is known as transcending comprehension and, therefore, empirical while in communion with the Triune God. The height, the precipitous mountain of the life in Christ, is principally the gift of the Spirit. "It is the Holy Spirit," says Basil, "who enlightens the path to the knowledge of God, inspires the prophets, gives wisdom to the legislators, leads the priests to perfection. If he receives a tax collector, he makes him an evangelist. If he enters into a fisherman, he makes him a theologian. If he finds a repentant persecutor, he makes him an apostle to the nations, a preacher of the faith, a vessel of election."[41]

[41]*Homily* 15 (PG 31.169).

God's Everlasting Presence

WHAT IN CONCRETE TERMS does the modern mind understand by Christ's incarnation? Although it is a mystery and will remain so forever, one can see its repercussions in daily life and history. The incarnation means that God came so near to us as to enable us to rise above ourselves and our human conditions and become like him. It means what Irenaeus of Lyons said: "God eternal became a Being in time, in order that we beings in time become eternal."[42] By such action, we enter into a new era, that of incorruptibility, of everlasting peace. Without such divine intervention, time and human existence would remain the most oppressing factors, spreading fear and horror, reminding us constantly of death and the absurdity of daily life.

Refusal of God's continuous presence or epiphany drives humanity back again to the narrow prison of time. Ignoring or disbelieving God's love (divine *philanthropia*), human beings return to time's dominating power. Man in our current language becomes a mere unit in an industrial and consumer society, assessed according to his productivity, his income, his earthly possessions, and not according to his spiritual values. Finally, two dates determine human existence: the birth date and the death date. So the weight of time without God's intervention is virtually unbearable. Although this intervention took place at a given time, that is at the beginning of the Christian era, it is a perpetual "present," linking forever man and God. Before us we have a "continuous now." The Christian experiences this incorruptible time during the "liturgical year" in the worshiping life of the church, the body of Christ. All the hymns sung in memory of the saints or in praise of the Eucharist underline a mystical presence, so that a past event seemingly takes place again before our eyes. Thus the consecration prayer says: "Hearken,

[42]Irenaeus of Lyons, *Against Heresies.*

O Lord and come, thou who sitteth above with the Father and art here invisibly present with us . . ."

No less than John Chrysostom himself described in this manner the saving stages of Christ's earthly life. In every Eucharist celebrated today, the same Jesus acts and saves:

> Believe, then, that too we are now concerned with that very same supper at which He himself sat. For this present one is in no way different from that one; neither is this the work of a man and that his work, but both this and that are his work. He who wrought the former also wrought the latter. When, therefore, you see the priest offering the sacrament to you, do not believe that it is the priest who is the agent, but that the outstretched hand is that of Christ. For just as in the case of baptism, it is not the priest who baptizes you, but God who holds your head with invisible force, and neither angel nor archangel nor anyone else dares to approach or touch it; so likewise is it at this moment. For when God brings to birth, he alone is capable of making this gift. Do you not see, regarding people who are about to arrange an adoption in this world, how they do not allow their servants to arrange the matter, but present themselves in person before the tribunal? In the same way, God has not given permission to the angels to offer the gift, but is present in his person, ordering all and saying: call no one your Father upon earth; not with a view to dishonoring your parents, but that you should set before all him who created you and placed you among his children. For he who made the ultimate offering, he who offered himself, will certainly not decline to offer you his own Body. Let us hear then, O Priests, and people under guidance, those things of which we have been judged worthy; let us listen and tremble; he gave it to be filled with his flesh, he offered himself in sacrifice. What then can be our excuse when, after such nourishment, we commit such sins? When, having eaten of the Lamb, we ourselves become wolves? When after having been fed from the Lamb we are as ravenous as lions? For this sacrament commands that we should be forever pure, not only of violence, but also of the least hostility.[43]

Although Christians can worship God in all places, from the very beginning there were assigned certain localities over which hovered the presence of the divine. Such places give concreteness and tangibility to faith and underline in particular the historical character of Christianity. Because the Eucharist is celebrated there, that place takes on a sacred character. Christ's incarnation justifies the con-

[43]*Homily* 50 *in Matthew*, n. 3 (PG 58.507–8).

sideration of appointed places of worship. The Liturgy of St. James included among its intercessions the following:

> We present our prayers to thee also, O Lord, for the holy places, which thou hast glorified by the divine appearing of thy Christ, and by the visitation of thy Holy Spirit; especially for the glorious Zion, mother of all the churches; and for thy holy, catholic and apostolic church throughout the world; even now, O Lord, bestow upon her the rich gifts of thy all Holy Spirit.

Being human with senses and legitimate demands, the assembly of the faithful obviously wants that place to satisfy certain conditions. The church building is not an ordinary building. Its use must be evident to the multitude who enter in. In his commentary on the *Sacra Liturgia,* Germanus, patriarch of Constantinople, rightly explains that: "it is earthly heaven wherein the heavenly God dwells and walks about."[44] Thus the faith of the worshipers in the reality beyond this world, in the truth of the spiritual world, has from the very beginning determined the content and style of her architecture and iconography.

Since God is the author of all creation, there has never been a sharp distinction between the sacred and the profane, between the physical and the metaphysical. Whatever was edifying was taken. John of Damascus said, "Let us seek out the wisdom of the profane. Perhaps we can find there something useful, and profit from something edifying for our souls."[45] The fathers felt no need to divide history and art into the secular and the sacred, for according to the historian Socrates "good, wherever it may be, belongs to one Truth."[46]

The fathers viewed history as a continuous linear process with no disruption in the divine economy. They did not raise the question, "What has Jerusalem to do with Athens?" The God of history before *anno Domini* is the same as the God of the Christian *historia.* The fathers emphasized the continuity of Christian culture with the Greek past. The new culture, the epiphany of the Logos, was simply the apex in a long process in the plan and historical involvement of God, who is never absent but who manifests his presence according to new situations and by the appropriate means.

[44]*Sacra Liturgica* (PG 98.384).
[45]John of Damascus, *The Fount of Wisdom* (PG 94.524–32).
[46]Socrates, *Church History* 111, 16.

God's Action in Time and Beyond Space and Time

TIME AND SPACE, in the context of relation between God and man, have been too much rationalized and absolutized—sometimes with mathematical precision—and have been seen as impenetrable obstacles between the Creator and the creation. We forget that for God all of these things are not applicable. Moreover, the terms used—immutability, activity, movement, etc.—are ours, and therefore they tend to lose their meaning. The lordship of God over the cosmos was minimized by arguing a colossal gap of impassable communication between God and man. An attempt was made to understand God according to our own measure and scientific criteria. Maximus the Confessor, however, stated that the ultimate aim of the descent of the Holy Spirit at Pentecost is the permanent union with the creatures, the union of the created with the Logos. Consequently, any other intervention of time as hindrance and of the natural law of growth are void. Nothing can prevent God from exercising his prerogatives as the Supreme Ruler of the universe.[47] Human beings are always marching toward the infinite, the beyond, the above, the highest, the unexpected—where time and distance cannot prevail. We feel that all events in the now, the present, are relative, phenomenal, temporal, incomplete. We are awaiting their perfection and completeness, their change into a new form in fullness, a meeting with the Absolute who alone can satisfy all which frustrates us. We revolt against the emptiness, nothingness, as meaningless when compared with the permanent and everlasting. A time misused, because of wrongly trying to fill it with dubious, unreliable, and unworthy deeds, does not lead to the *real life* but to death. The simple reason is that man in such a situation does not get out of his moral self; he is not entering, therefore, into communion with the true "other," with God who is the absolute person, the abso-

[47]*Quaestiones ad Thalassium* (PG 90.760).

lute source of life, filling and satisfying all. Regarding the subject of *chronos,* time as the servant of death, Basil of Caesarea rightly stated:

> In fact, there did exist something, as it seems, even before the world, to which our mind can attain by contemplation but which has been left uninvestigated because it is not adapted to those who are beginners and as yet infants in understanding. This was a certain condition older than the birth of the world and proper to the supramundane powers, one beyond time, everlasting, without beginning or end. In it the Creator and Producer of all things perfected the works of his art, a spiritual light befitting the blessedness of those who love the Lord, rational and invisible natures, and the whole orderly arrangements of spiritual creatures which surpass our understanding and of which it is impossible even to discover the names. These fill completely the essence of the indivisible world as Paul teaches us when he says "For in him were created all things" whether visible or invisible . . . When at length, it was necessary for this world also to be added to what already existed, primarily as a place of training and a school for the souls of men, then was created a fit dwelling place for all things in general which are subject to birth and destruction . . . In truth, is this not the nature of time, whose past has vanished, whose future is not yet at hand, and whose present escapes perception before it is known?[48]

Basil here follows Aristotle: "Beginning means that part of a thing from which one would start first; that from which each thing would best be originated; that from which, as an immanent part, a thing first comes to be; for example, change naturally first begins —and so are the arts, and of these especially the architectonic arts, called beginnings."[49]

The human mind has always been frustrated and in a continuous embarrassment regarding God's activity of creating from nothing. It is difficult to understand such a process for the simple reason that, surrounded by a material world which is already created, we hardly understand that there was a time when it did not exist. We tend to believe in an eternal form of matter. Early philosophers gave different interpretations, assuming that through a long evolution things came out of a primitive nucleus of matter. Whatever scientists may conclude, there still is complete mystery as to the very origin of the visible creation. The Book of Genesis tells us in

[48]Basil of Caesarea, *Homilies in Hexaemeron* 1, 5 (PG 29.13).
[49]*Metaphysics* 5, 1, 1012b.

condensed wording that God created the visible and invisible things from nothing. Theodoret of Cyrus, writing in 429, was aware of such problematics of the creation, even that of time as having an origin. In dealing with adversaries of the Christian faith who had a Greek intellectual background, Theodoret remarks, "God needs nothing, while human endeavors need each other's contribution . . . But the Creator of the universe does not need either instruments or matter. What for other artists is matter, instrument, labor, time, science, and attentive care, for the God of all is the will."[50]

For Basil of Caesarea, time is this interspace inseparable from the idea of the world even to such an extent as to coincide with the creation: *Chronos de estin to symparekteinomenon tē systasei tou kosmou diastēma.*[51] Basil already knew the scientific conceptions of the ancient world of cyclic movements. Because of such cyclic movements, we must not conclude that the creation is without beginning. In fact, Sextus Empiricus,[52] Chalcidius,[53] and John of Lydia[54] taught this cyclic, eternal moving of the universe. Aristotle, relying on the circular movement of stars,[55] proved the eternity of the sky. But Basil is satisfied to repeat such arguments and images of eternity in order to proceed to another chapter, refuting them and proving that the circle starts from a point—therefore, inevitably having a first movement and beginning.

Gregory of Nyssa repeats the same argument[56] that movement means the first cause of movement. Elsewhere Basil, inspired by Aristotle,[57] states that where something is created and born, inevitably there also exists anticipated destruction. In fact, Aristotle believed in the eternity of the material world: "That the heaven as a whole neither came into being nor admits of destruction, as some assert, but is one and eternal, with no end or beginning . . . we may convince ourselves."[58]

But such ideas of an eternal world lead to pantheism or identify-

[50]*Graecorum affectionum curatio* 114 (PG 83.916).
[51]*Adversus Eunomium* 1, 21 (PG 29.560).
[52]*Adversus Mathematicos* 3, 107.
[53]*Commentary on Timacus* 68.
[54]*De Mensa* 3, 3.
[55]*Physics* 8, 8, 264.
[56]*De opificio hominis* 23 (PG 44.209).
[57]*De Caelo* 1, 12, 288b.
[58]*De Caelo* 2, 1, 283b.

ing the created world with the Supreme Being, as is attested by Origen: "The Greeks say plainly that the world on the whole is God; the Stoics, that it is the first God; the followers of Plato, that it is the second; but some of them that it is the third."[59]

Time and world are two correlative and inseparable notions. Time begins with the creation of the universe. This universe was not made during time but with the parallel creation of time. So time did not exist before. What coincides, therefore, with the creation of the world, is condemned to change, to decline, to reduction, and to final annihilation. Since the world is finite like all creatures, Athanasius of Alexandria remarks that:

> It is the property of created things not to exist before their becoming, so that they come out of nothing and they have a beginning in their creation; only the Logos of God, in contrast to creatures which started to become, has no beginning in his existence and certainly should not begin to exist; because as the Father who has begotten him is eternal, he is also eternal. Created things cannot enjoy eternity, since they have a beginning in existence, they are taken from nothing and they did not exist before becoming. All these which have not existed before they became, how would they coexist with God who exists always? Consequently, those who claim the eternity of creation are led to the same irrationalism and foolishness with those who contest the eternity of the Lord of the creation and Logos of God.[60]

In the same sense Maximus the Confessor reflects the patristic view by saying:

> Some claim the eternal coexistence of creatures with God, which is quite impossible. Because, how can being, in all points limited, coexist for eternity with Him who is absolutely infinite? Or how can that which is substantially created be coeternal with the Creator? That which has been produced from nothing into being cannot in fact become coeternal with what is without beginning and has always existed.[61]

In God's attribute of creative energies, we must assume that there is no change in his very nature. God is Creator eternally and supra-

[59]*Contra Celsum* 5, 581.

[60]*Contra Arianos* 2, 1, 22 (PG 26.148, 193, 269; *Epistula encyclica ad episcopos Aegypti et Libyae* 8 (PG 26.1044).

[61]*Four Centuries on Charity* 4, 6 (PG 90.1049).

temporally because he has in himself all that constitutes the Creator, namely, the will to conceive a plan, to modify it, to execute it, and to take after-care.

An acceptance of evolution moves toward a mechanistic interpretation of the universe and of mankind. Creation, on the other hand, demands the introduction of the supernatural; this is abhorrent to anyone who accepts only scientific data. The scientists must work out processes. Conversely, the "creationist" defends the idea of an eternal God who works in eternity as well as in time, who is personal and who deals with men personally, and who is, therefore, not only the "I am" but also the God of revelation and communicability with his creation. The word "evolution" demands that what now appears is already in the system of the potential out of which it evolves. Nothing else is demanded; anything more than this leads to confusion.

There always remains a large area of discussion on the question: how does God who is Spirit relate to matter? Creation "out of nothing" is a mystery. Creative process working on matter is also a deep mystery. If God creates, he creates out of nothing. The question becomes very pressing in the relationship between divine sovereignty and human freedom. To say that such areas are shrouded in mystery is in no way to deny their reality. Rather, it is to assert that if evidence is derived from a study of the material world according to law and order, then there is no scientific answer to the theological question. In brief, a Christian is forced again and again into belief rather than "evidence." Epistemologically, we must insist that beginnings for the scientists have to be an assumption, an acceptance in faith. Much of what follows for the scientist is because he believes in the strength of his hypostasis. And much of what follows for a Christian is because he believes that there is a God who not only is able to act on the matter he created, but also does act. We see through a glass darkly, and it is time that we face the cloudy fact.

By the liturgical act, the celebrant repeats what is enacted in heaven and by the high priest, Christ; this ideal performance of Eucharist in heaven is mirrored in the sanctuary where the Lord, represented by the officiant, receives the sacred gifts carried in holy fear by the deacons dressed as angels. In the liturgical hymn "All mortal flesh keep silence," the sacred emotion arises through the dematerialized forms of the angels and the actual "silence of the flesh," as worship itself especially demands at the entrance of the sacred gifts. When the worshiper sees these otherworldly forms which the skill and style of liturgical art created, his whole being is moved by the realization that truly "the powers of heaven worship invisible with us."

The application of the exhortation to worship of the human body, "think of nothing earthly in itself . . . ," would certainly not have been helped by the presentation of angels and saints, who would have brought to mind not divine but altogether earthly persons. This exhortation alone is capable of signifying the character of Orthodox piety. The whole setting—iconography, sacred music, architectural style, vestments, etc.—seeks to create a climate which reminds one of "nothing earthly."

Time in worship is not measured as the natural flow of events, that is, the past, the present, and the future; in worship the past and the future are regarded as the immediate present. Time ceases to exist and is changed into a mystical experience of life in which eternity is lived in the present. The things of the past and of the future and even the eschatological things, prehistory and the main stages of the redemptive work of Christ as well as the salutary gifts extending to the last days which flowed from him, are condensed and lived mystically as present before us. Each sign of the saving work of the Lord is relived through the lifting of the concept of time. The individual events of religious history should not be understood as mere occurrences but as part of a mystic plan which is valid even today. This means that the worshiper does not merely recall, but lives and actually partakes of the life of the Savior and of the communion of saints.

Sacred persons and events, from the Bible or from church history, are likewise represented in such a manner that they are "contemporized" and appear to belong to the eternal present—or to eternity introduced and lived in the present and at every moment of time. In Orthodox worship a historical event from the life of Christ or the apostles that takes place within a closed space—as, for example, the annunciation, the salutation of Elizabeth by the Mother of God, the Last Supper—is represented as if it had taken place outside of this space. The very character of Christ's continuous redeeming power, the constant pressure of his Spirit in his church, visibly manifests the spiritual significance of the represented historical events as beyond space and time. They are outside the limitations of space and time and have so acquired an infinite extension and duration. Martyrs and confessors are raised to the continuous present by being released from those unnecessary human elements which would have characterized and emphasized only their past significance.

In this way, the believer is not prevented from feeling that the narrated events could take place even today and that, consequently, the passion and the resurrection constitute fundamental subjects not only of the past but also of the present. Thus, present-tense expressions or the adverb "today" are often used. Episodes from Christ's public ministry—baptism, theophany, epiphany, the outpouring of his Spirit—are dramatized as events of this moment, as "now." Christ being the same yesterday, today, and forever (Heb. 13:8) comes even today to us through worship as he came also to his contemporaries. As an example, let us take a few extracts from the Liturgy:

> Today the Virgin gives birth to the Creator . . .
> Today he hangs on a beam . . .
> Today Hades bemoaning cries . . .
> Today salvation has been made for the world;
>   let us sing unto the Risen One . . .

The *kenosis* of Christ upon the cross is sung as though enacted today, thus as overcoming the limits of time; those who receive Communion worthily are deified ethically by participation in the divine. Communicants break through time's barriers and are led to the "soul-feeding table" (*psychotrophon trapezan*). Christ is not labeled as the "sacrificed one" (*o tythis*) but (*o thiomenos*) as "the one being sacrificed." In relation to the Eucharist, "the Lamb of God is cut into pieces and distributed" (*melizetai kai diamerizetai o amnos tou Theou*).

Liturgy and iconography reflect the ethos and the depth of Orthodox theology. Accordingly, God is the Father and Pantocrator; the Son stands beside him as being consubstantial; the Mother of God is an expression of the incarnation of the Logos; and the saints, citizens of heaven, are "clothed in the glory not of earthly but of celestial things." Christ is not presented as a "beautiful" man, for this would be a Nestorian heresy, overemphasizing the human nature in relation to the hypostatic union of God-man. Both his divinity and his cohonorable (*omotimos*) body are exalted. The crucifixion is likewise portrayed in such a manner as not to arouse pity for human suffering, but rather awe at the power of divine love—the self-emptying of the inexhaustible.

Through the ages, the eyes of the faithful have clearly witnessed the eternal, invisible transcendent order. Like St. Paul, an earlier visionary, they looked "not to the things that are seen but to the things that are unseen" (2 Cor. 4:18). Unshakeable faith and intense mystic contemplation have sustained their vision of the divine. They have shared that vision with all Byzantium. Their ears have rung with celestial melodies intoned by angels circling the throne of God, according to the vision of the prophet Isaiah (6:1–3). These are their models. When they sing, they sing in harmony with those songs. The Byzantines took very literally the words "on earth as in heaven." Their hymns united earth to heaven in one harmonious cosmic song of praise to the Creator of the universe. The faithful were delighted to recall as an example of such harmony how the shepherds, humble earthlings, sang together with flaming angels when Christ was born, "Beings of fire sang hymns together with creatures of clay."[62]

Much of this liturgical poetry is sung in the Eucharist, actualizing through the imagery of language, gesture, chant, and invocation the original mystery of the incarnation and the resurrection. No church so lavishly employs poetry as does the Eastern Orthodox. The fact that poetry constitutes three-fourths of the Divine Liturgy accounts in a large part for its powerful emotional and aesthetic appeal. In the early centuries these poetic sermons called *kontakia,* set to music and sung, displaced prose sermons and were, therefore, delivered by the deacons from the pulpit after the Scripture readings.

The poetic trappings of worship remind one of the earliest account of the activity of the Muses in Greek antiquity. Hesiod, the epic poet,[63] describes how the Muses, the daughters of Zeus and

[62]Romanos Melodos, *Nativity Kontakion* 12, 4.
[63]*Theogony* 22–34.

Mnemosyne, came to him while he herded sheep on the holy mountain Helicon. They taught him beautiful songs and gave him a
marvelous staff of flowering olive. They "breathed into me a divine
voice that I might celebrate things of the past and the future. They
ordered me to hymn the race of blessed, immortal gods, and first
and always to sing of them."[64]

Each account relates an actual experience of the faithful. In each
case mystic communion takes place between the person and the divine. From experience comes new inspiration, confidence, and
strength. The worshiper assumes the sacred duty of singing hymns
to God. He is henceforth a poet with a mission and responsibility.

Obedient to the Muses's command, the worshiper's soul and lips
will breathe out God. Each of the hymns will be a true offertory,
which Plato defined as "a kind of ode, prayer to the gods."[65] Plato
declares that the only writers he would allow in the ideal city
would be writers of hymns to the gods and *enkomia* to good
men.[66] Doxology, the song of adoration, has first place in any inter-
course with God. The faithful believer stands in the liturgical attitude with hands and heart uplifted and sings the hymn. He faces
God, addressing him directly. In ecstatic lyrics and in a mass of
metaphor, superlative, paradox, and sacred emotion, he attempts to
praise what he knows to be beyond man's comprehension and
speech, God's infinite power, wisdom, and love.

> Thou the perfect image of the incomprehensible hypostasis
>   of the Father, the unapproachable Light,
>   the exact seal of divinity, the brightness of glory,
>   illuminating the souls of men in truth,
> Thou art he who existeth before all ages and who created
>   the universe.
> For thou art a far-shining light, the Light of thy Father
>   unmingled, unlimited and beyond comprehension, even though,
>   thou didst become man, O only Friend of Man.[67]

His profound mystical awareness of the Absolute articulated in
these hymns shatters the barriers between heaven and earth, thereby
enabling the souls of others to rise and contemplate the immutable
glory of God, as we see in Romanos's case:

[64]Ibid., 31–34.
[65]*Laws* 700b.
[66]*Republic* 607a.
[67]Romanos, *Fourth Kontakion* VI, 2–9.

And with the eyes of his soul,
    He saw the legions of archangels and angels,
    standing in fear and praising Christ.[68]

Doxology not only provides a landscape for the faithful, but it also symbolizes the eternal reality of the spiritual realm which alone exalts and gives purpose to human life. From all such texts a dynamic image of God emerges. He is the eternally active Creator of the universe, its majestic ruler (*basileus*), the Pantocrator who looks down from the domes of Byzantine churches. But above all, God is the one true friend of man. He is indeed *philanthropos*. Out of this love God took on flesh and became man so that man could become God. This is the universal theme of all Byzantine sacred poetry. To continue the dialogue which has begun between the Father in heaven and his children on earth, God turns from the joyful vision of eternity and addresses man. Here he uses either the second person or the first person plural, identifying himself with the whole Christian family.

The inspired hierophant, illumined by the light of the knowledge of God, possesses a wisdom (*sophia*) greater than that of other men. He knows what has passed, is passing, or is to come—that is to say, all the parts of God's design and will. The Orthodox firmly believe that such a divine design has always existed. They are equally confident that man's spirit could penetrate beyond the confusion of the phantom, material world to discover it. They are aware of God's plan for man's return to Paradise. Man is nourished with the hope of eternal life, resurrection, and final deification, and even the *theōsis* of the entire cosmos. The words *zoe* and *anastasis* sound loudly and often in Orthodox hymnography. "Through thy goodness Thou hast become the Life and Resurrection of all."[69]

In other hymns, the worshiper is less emotional. He has descended from heaven to earth and seeks immediate communication with his brethren. This means that the voice of God is heard on earth. God responds to the doxology. The Creator and creature converse with each other. Lifting his arms to heaven, as does the Theotokos in the Deisis, he petitions God for continued blessings. The petitions may

[68]Ibid., 4, 5, 4.
[69]*Kontakion* IV, 16, 1.

be specifically for the church, rulers, deliverance from natural dis-
asters, or general in character:

> To thee we pray, all-holy One, who has endured suffering,
> Thou art life, restoration and the fountain of all goodness,
> Look down from heaven and succor all those who trust thee,
> From wrath, and calamity and sorrow deliver our lives,
> O Lord, and guide all in the faith of truth,
> through the intercession of the Theotokos and virgin,
> Save the world which is thine, save thy flock, preserve
> all mankind,
> Thou who for our sakes didst become, without change, man,
> The only Friend of man.[70]

Orthodox hymns mediate between God and man. Like the angels
on Jacob's ladder, they come and go between heaven and earth,
uniting spirit and matter within the folds of song. Indeed, it is the
work of the angels to glorify God in music and to carry his Word
to man. The Orthodox worshiper is a lover of beauty, a soul in pur-
suit of God. He rejoices in man's loyalty and in God's mercy, which
he asks to intervene and to enable him to live worthily:

> O savior, may my deadened soul arise again with thee,
>   May sorrow not destroy her and may she not ever
>   forget these songs which sanctify her.
> Yea, O merciful One, do not pass by me, sullied
>   though I be by many sins. O my Father, holy and
>   compassionate, may thy name be forever hallowed
>   in my mouth and on my lips,
>   in my voice and in my songs.
> Grant grace to me when I proclaim thy hymns, for
>   thou hast the power, who offerest resurrection to
>   fallen man.[71]

[70]*Kontakion* IV, 18, 1.
[71]*Kontakion* 29, 24, 1–5.

The Effects of
Christ's Incarnation

THE CHRISTOLOGICAL CONFLICTS appeared in the early church as a natural consequence of the deep concern as to how ordinary man can overcome the iniquities of the post-Adamic situation and become better than he actually is. In other words, is it possible for man to enter again into a filial relationship, to reach God, and to become a new creature like Christ? Is Christ an attainable model to be followed or is sinful nature unconquerable, so strong that man resists in vain, wrestles in vain, being condemned forever to remain under the dominion of his fallen nature and hopelessly unaided?

In the early centuries, such problems deeply preoccupied many Christian thinkers. St. Augustine refuted Pelagius who claimed that man is desperately wounded; he cannot be different from what he is since he is completely and irreparably ruined and deformed. And thus, the theology of grace was developed at length. Many people have felt that the divine element within us is too weak and, therefore, is not sufficient for overcoming the earthly element. Hence, a legitimate question arose: what is the connection between this investigation and Christ's incarnation? If man cannot be uplifted and restored to his ancient glory, then Christ's purpose in coming down to earth and in imparting humanity is in vain and completely irrelevant to our tragic situation.

The fathers immediately saw the intimate relationship between the doctrine of Christ's epiphany and actual human life and reality. So they affirmed that Christ's incarnation in God's economy aimed precisely at helping man to attain a better life. All the stages of his redemptive work aimed at man's pursuance of the eternal model (*typos*) put before him by his teaching. Christ, being exactly of the same nature as all human beings and not imaginary, conquered temptations and overcame death.

St. Athanasius and the Council of Nicaea established the church's faith in the full divinity of Jesus Christ. As the discussions about the

three persons in the unity of the Godhead were coming to a generally agreed conclusion, the argument turned to the way in which
divinity and humanity were united in the one person of Christ.
Here agreement proved to be very difficult indeed, owing to the
differing ways in which people approached this question.

There were in general two lines of approach to the problem. One
was to emphasize the *unity* of the person of Christ above everything else; the other was to emphasize *the reality of both the
humanity and the divinity* in him. The theological leaders of Alexandria took the first of these two lines of approach, and the School of
Antioch took the second line of approach. To complicate matters
further, considerable confusion arose because many people did not
see any distinction between "nature" and "person." In some of the
languages which Christians of those days used, it was practically
impossible to represent the difference between "nature" and "person," as was done in philosophical Greek by the terms *physis* and
hypostasis. Even in Greek, the distinctions between *ousia* and
physis and between *hypostasis* and *prosōpon* were not always clear,
so misunderstandings were almost inevitable.

Apollinaris followed the Alexandrian line of thought. In his eagerness to maintain both the divinity of Christ and the unity and integrity of his personality, Apollinaris taught that Jesus had "the
body and the animal soul" of a man, but that "the reasoning spirit
in him" was the Logos, that is, the second person of the Trinity.
This meant, in actual effect, a denial of the full humanity of Christ,
and the church condemned this teaching at the Council of Constantinople in A.D. 381.

Nestorius followed the Antiochene line of thought and asserted
the distinctness of the divinity and the humanity in Jesus Christ.
In his eagerness to emphasize the real and full humanity of Christ,
he tended to lose sight of the inseparable union of divinity and
humanity in the person of Christ. It *seemed*, according to Nestorius,
that Jesus was only a "God-bearing man" or "a man energized by
the Logos of God," and that the divinity and the humanity in him
could be separated. Whether Nestorius actually meant to teach this
in this particular form, this view nevertheless came to be known as
Nestorianism and was condemned by the Council of Ephesus in
A.D. 431.

Although Apollinarianism and Nestorianism were thus condemned by ecumenical councils of the church, the discussion regarding the union of the Godhead and manhood in the person of Christ did not come to an end there. Eutychius, a monk of Constantinople, in his eagerness to denounce Nestorianism declared that Jesus Christ was indeed formed *out of* the union of the two natures, human and divine, but that *after* the union there was only one nature in him, and it was divine. This was going beyond what Cyril and the other Alexandrian theologians had said.

The theory that man has power enough to be able to save himself was combated by all the doctors of the church. Epiphanius, a famous theologian and deacon of Catania, developed this point with profound insight.

As a result of the intervention of sin our fragile nature is not what it once was. This explains why man, since he is fallen, cannot attain the dignity of the first Adam. Human nature, being as it is, has need of a nobler force strong enough to be irresistible. Only such a power can succeed in overcoming the stains that stem from our weakness of will. By contributing its additional and extraordinary power, it will enable us to become strong enough to prevent any relapse. The whole choir of prophets, moved by the Holy Spirit, had foreknowledge of the gift that was promised and that was to be forthcoming. Each, in accordance with his time and particular circumstances, foretold the giving of such a blessing and linked it with the proclamation of the revelation of the consubstantial, blessed and coeternal Trinity—Father, Son and Holy Ghost. Because of the abundance of God's goodness he humbled himself, came down and took upon himself our manhood. Having once taken our nature upon himself, he condescended to restore it to its original dignity by means of the invisible and immaterial fire of his divinity.[72]

However, man receives in Christ—the Logos made man—an intimate share in what is divine: life everlasting and incorruptible. The main characteristic of *theōsis* is, according to the fathers, precisely immortality (*athanasia*) or incorruption (*aphtharsia*). Only the word *theōsis* can adequately render the uniqueness of the promise and the offer.

This term *theōsis* is indeed quite embarrassing, if we would think in ontological terms and categories. There is no doubt that man simply cannot become god, even through Promethean actions. But

[72]*Panegyzical Sermon* (PG 98.1316).

the fathers were thinking in personal terms every time they referred
to divinization. The mystery of personal communication was involved at this point. *Theōsis* meant a personal encounter. The
sanctification of man is rather offensive to the modern ear. This is
difficult for many to grasp, with their iconoclastic desire to uproot
any hint of idolatry. But *theōsis* remains the restoration of man
from mortality to immortality; it means that the communicant is
offered the means whereby he may return to his original relationship
with God. Thus is realized the promise given in the Old Testament:
"I say, 'You are gods, sons of the Most High, all of you'" (Ps. 82:6).
In brief, salvation is not primarily the restitution of a broken legal
relationship that has been upset by sin. Rather, it is the fulfillment,
renewal, transfiguration, perfection, and deification of man's whole
being.

The hypostatic union of the two divine and human natures of
Jesus has another implication with reference to human behavior
and especially to our will and our liberty. That is why saints and
ascetics continuously fight above all to subdue their deficient will
and thus to make it free from any carnal desire and sensual earthly
dominion. The more the will is liberated from material attachments,
the more it copies Christ, since he had submitted his own will to
that of his Father. In this renunciation of the natural will, the
product of our fallen post-Adamic nature, real freedom is accomplished by a free "person." The appropriation of a healthy will implies the evacuation and rejection of the evil one. Only then can
such a human being contain Christ, this divine person, because the
perfect life, according to Gregory of Nyssa, is the "imitation of
God's nature."[73] Maximus the Confessor adds that "the supreme object of the saints is not only to be united with the Holy Trinity, but
to express it in a most concrete way, and to imitate it within their
own lives."[74] Christ renders to every man all the powers and capacities needed so that he may follow and copy the example of his
prototype, thus becoming an antitype, an image of the divinity. If
God is incomparable and beyond our reach, our human heart nevertheless contains something unique which nostalgically seeks, waits,
and expects its Creator. It is a homeward journey. Gregory of Nyssa
rightly says in this respect: "We hide within us something which

---

[73]*De professione christiana* (PG 46.244).
[74]*Ambigua* (PG 91.1196).

causes us to resemble God, to participate in God; it is indispensable to possess in our being something which conforms us to participation in him."[75]

In this twofold movement leading to the most blessed meeting, otherwise a synergism, we discover the optimistic approach of Orthodox soteriology. This mainly proceeds from the deep consciousness that man, in spite of his vicissitudes, remains forever the *imago Dei,* thus opposing gnostic fatalism, the obsession and anguish caused by the theory of predestination, and the obscure view of the unfortunate *massa damnata.* Orthodoxy has never been touched by the Pelagian deviation as has Western Christianity. Our fallen nature, profoundly vulnerable, cannot overcome its limitations unless it is sustained by a salutary intervention of divine action. Commenting on the parable of the lost drachma, Nicolas Cabasilas remarks: "It is the Master who has stooped toward the earth, thus refinding his image."[76] Original sin, it is true, considerably weakened man's creative capacity for godly actions. While it had obscured the relationship, it did not completely efface the image, which is why Christ found his own image again in man. The fathers in their inquiry into grace warn of the danger of confusing the free will of intention with the acts. While St. Augustine taught *"Non posse non peccare,"* they warn of various forms of endemic Pelagianism and affirm the complete freedom of the will and its capacity to say the "fiat"—the desire for salvation and renewal.

If we insist so much on the effects of the incarnation, it is because a Christian, through mystical union with Christ, appropriates all of Christ's divine qualities concerning victory over evil and death and corruptibility. Indeed, by such elevation man becomes an otherworldly creature already during this earthly life. The future of history, therefore, belongs to such men of faith and prayer because only such people possess the answers, whereas others faced with upheavals or desperate economic or social problems see only in an impasse, darkness, and despair. Humanistic sciences suffer from a certain determinism, which limits the scope for hope of a final solution. A Christian, from this point of view, is a man of the impossible because he finds a way out, a safe exit, a light, never yielding to exterior conditions and obstacles. He sees beyond the border, the

[75]*Oratio Catechetica* 5 (PG 91.1196).
[76]*The Life in Christ.*

human horizon. He possesses that secret power about which Christ said that it may remove even mountains and all kind of obstacles (Matt. 17:21).

All martyrs and confessors succeeded in breaking through human limitations and overcoming weaknesses, adversities, and all kinds of hindrances. They were in this respect wonderworkers, not by their own merits, but by the mighty link with Christ who in an invisible way makes all his members deified, "christified," able to do what the world thinks is impossible. Indeed, behind their achievements lies an invisible source of might and faith. This "plus" of believers constitutes the main superiority over fearful and despairing people. The true Christian lives in complete confidence in God's mercy and in a continuous chain of *Kyrie eleison*. Thence, he feels in security, in peace, and protected by God's love, while others are in panic.

Deepening their reflections on Christ's humanity, the fathers offered further thoughts that directly concern all of us. If Christ, as a man, lived through daily reality without yielding to temptations and, although attacked by Satan, succeeded in overcoming those attacks, it follows that man too, of whatever age or situation, can dominate his self and withstand the pressure of satanic powers. This is so because of the intimate relationship between those who are united with Christ through baptism and Eucharist. With such eyes one has to see the membership of the church, that is, of his mystical body, in a dynamic and creative way and not in a static and passive one.

This is made clear in the fight against Monothelitism, a seventh-century heresy confessing only one will in the God-man. In the well-known "Ecthesis" drawn up by Sergius, patriarch of Constantinople, mention is made of one or two energies but of only one will in Christ. Because of the many irregularities threatening the orthodoxy of this statement, Emperor Constans II (648) later issued another document, the so-called "Typos." In it he rejected both the monothelitic and the dyothelitic formulas. The controversy was finally settled by the Council of Constantinople in 680, which condemned the monothelitic formula and proclaimed the existence of the wills in Christ, divine and human, to be the orthodox faith. Theologically, the issues at stake in the controversy were very similar to those raised by Monophysitism.

From the hypostatic union of the two natures in Christ stem certain doctrinal consequences: the *perichoresis* or interpenetrations of the two natures. This means that the dwelling or cohabitation of the two natures is made without confusion. Each one has retained its own attributes without alteration. As in the Holy Trinity, where we accept one substance but three hypostases entering into the others without confusion or losing their identities, so likewise in the case of Christ we accept one hypostasis in two natures being united hypostatically and intercommunicating-*perichorousas* between them, without any change occurring. In Christ this *perichoresis* is exceptional in that the divine nature enters into his humanity but not the reverse. If the sun in transmitting us its rays remains untouched by our state, how much more does this occur with the Creator and Lord of the sun, asks John of Damascus.[77]

Jesus Christ reveals to us and renders possible this knowledge of the Father: "The Logos of God became visible with a body so that we can have some idea of the invisible Father."[78] Out of such new knowledge of God emerges the imperative duty to achieve moral renewal and the reorientation of our daily attitude:

> Whoever wants to understand discourse on the subject of God has to be purified in this manner in his daily life and become similar to the saints through the similarity of his individual actions. In such a way, united to them in the behavior of his own life, he may be able to understand all that has been revealed by God to us.[79]

By reconciling Christology and the main mission of his death and resurrection to all believers, we see that Christ makes available the fruits of the cross and resurrection to all. For this purpose, he established the church on earth, that is, his body, by transmitting all he has promised in the sacramental life in order to obtain full *koinonia* with God. In such a way, we are transported to the very heart of the Christian event: redemption by the action of Christ, the radical renewal of man, restored according to the image and the similitude of God, and the reestablishment of the communion of life between man and God. In this way, a profound ethical change, touching the core of our being, is taking place—the fruit of reconciliation and fellowship with God. Like all divine truths, Christology has too often been a matter for argument instead of a living posses-

[77]*The Orthodox Faith* 3, 7.
[78]Ibid.
[79]Ibid.

sion. It might be thought that God, having once humbled himself to appear in human form, would stay visible on earth. Indeed, the Gospel record shows that it was so expected. "We have heard from the law that the Christ remains for ever. How can you say that the Son of man must be lifted up?" (John 12:34). The disciples needed to go through the dark valley of his absence before they could know the fullness of his presence. Then the concentrated manifestation of God Incarnate could work in them. The Spirit could teach them all things and bring all things to their remembrance concerning whatsoever he had taught them. We can only know Christ intimately by partaking of his nature, by obtaining his Spirit.

In Athanasius of Alexandria (295–373) the soteriological doctrine has an important place. His *De Incarnatione Verbi* deals with the question of man's redemption. It has been said that Athanasius speaks of salvation only in terms of Christ's incarnation in the narrow sense. It cannot be denied that Athanasius lays stress on Christ's incarnation in the narrow sense as the means by which man's nature is united with the divine, elevated and deified, and that this is what he means when he writes: "God became man, that we might become gods." However, I think that this teaching does not represent the whole Athanasian doctrine of salvation. In his treatise on incarnation, Athanasius expressed his full conception of salvation.

> The Logos, knowing that the corruption of men could not be undone unless at all costs there was death, and because it was not possible for the Logos to die (being immortal and the Son of the Father), for this reason he takes to himself a body than can die so that this body, participating in the Logos who is above all, may become liable to death on behalf of all, and on account of the indwelling Logos may remain immortal, and in future corruption may cease in all by the grace of his resurrection. Whence, as a victim and a sacrifice free from all blemish, carrying into death the body which he took unto himself, he made death disappear in all its forms by the offering of an equivalent . . . and thus the incorruptible Son of God, dwelling with all through similar attributes. fittingly clothed all with incorruptibility in the promise of his resurrection.[80]

As we can see, the incarnation, death, and resurrection of Christ are here linked together, and it is only in terms of all of them that

[80]*De Incarnatione Verbi* 22.

Athanasius speaks of salvation. Death would be impossible without presupposing the reality of the incarnation. All of the events of Christ's earthly life are inseparable. The benefits of salvation are expounded in the life of our Savior taken as a whole. All of our sufferings were laid on him who could not suffer, and he destroyed them. "He destroyed death by death and all human weakness by his human actions." This is the way to understand the representative character of Christ's death and sacrifice and the possibility of man's salvation in Christ. Christ was born for us, lived on earth for us, died for us, and rose for us and for the confirmation of our resurrection. Christ's death was not due to his weakness but to the fact that he died for man's salvation.[81] While Athanasius speaks of the incarnation and insists that "God became man that we might become gods,"[82] he says at the same time that "Christ offered the sacrifice on behalf of all, delivering his own shrine to death in place of all, that he might set all free from the liability of the original transgression," and he speaks of Christ's sacrifice offered for the redemption of our sins[83] and for men's deliverance from corruption.[84] For Athanasius, Christ's death retains a place of importance in the plan of salvation. Immortality came to men through death.[85] Christ paid our debt for us. In Athanasius we meet with the synthesis of the two ideas of immortality or reconstitution of our nature and the idea of expiation of our death.

It is true that in the *Confessio Augustana* the First Article affirms the *Christus pro nobis* thesis and the fact of the two natures of Christ. He remains real man and real God. Besides the deity of Christ, there is also his humanity expressed in the words "became man, born of the pure virgin Mary," thus reaffirming the Nicene christological doctrine.

But Christology without implementing the impact of the hypostatic union in earthly reality, in history, and in the life of believers remains inoperative, disincarnate, and without any direct soteriological impact. Early Christianity saw in this theandric union a permanent relationship between the saving action of the Logos and the community of believers. The saving action is articulated by the

[81]Ibid.
[82]Ibid., 54.
[83]*Contra Arianos* 11, 7.
[84]*De Incarnatione Verbi* 9, 1.
[85]*Contra Arianos* 2, 66.

Holy Spirit in the church through visible means, being visible precisely because the invisible Logos has been made flesh, visible, incarnate. Any isolated approach to Christ's incarnation diminishes
his continuous mission in the world, and the role of the church as
"the ark of salvation" becomes marginal, obscure, and meaningless.
His reign is "forever, to the ages unto the ages."

Christ is not a Savior belonging to the past of long ago only, but
everlastingly our constant redeemer. Such a view contradicts the
ephapax (once and for all) sacrifice on the cross and his triumph
over death, sin, the law, and God's wrath. The fact of the redemption, that Christ gave "his life as a ransom for many" (Matt. 20:
28), is at the center of the church's faith. The more deeply we
pierce into the doctrine of the incarnation, the more we see its
dimensions and continuity within the community of the redeemed
through the appropriate channels, as understood and experienced
immediately after Pentecost when the first disciples shared in proclaiming the Word of God and breaking the eucharistic bread
(Acts 2:42).

Such a relationship of Christ with his believers explains the pour-
ing out of special blessings on them. Thus, the glorification of the
virgin Mary was made possible only through the humiliation of the
Son. Through the virgin the Son of God became the Son of man,
and through the Son, Mary became the Mother of God and received the "glory which belongs to God." The Theotokos is the
first human being to take part in the final deification of all creation.
The Orthodox hymn of the feast of her dormition is sung as
follows:

> The whole world was amazed at your divine glory: for you, O virgin
> who did not know wedlock have been translated from earth to the
> eternal mansions and to life without end, bestowing salvation upon
> all who sing your praises.

The relevant hymns do not narrate the feast as an isolated historical event but involve all humanity in its significance and its glory.

No view of life takes sin more seriously than does the Christian
view. Yet it regards evil as an additive, something with which man
has contaminated life but something which God can and does remove through Christ's incarnation. Thus the Christian can admit
the full dimensions of evil and yet greet life with an affirmative and

optimistic attitude. For him to be alive is a blessing, a divine gift to be enjoyed. Life is not a curse but a chance to enter into God's kingdom. At the heart of reality is a transcendent divine goodness that created the world good and is greater than all of the world's acquired sin and death.

With the psalmist, a Christian sees the growing grass as a sign and guarantee that the mercy of God endures forever. At the eucharistic offering, we see the climax of redemption, the room that the divine grace makes for the sparrow; for at the altar of God, the sparrow finds a place to build her nest and raise her young. It is not true that the nature of our sin must first be learned from pessimistic thinkers. Our sin can be understood only within the Christian forgiveness of the cross. Outside of forgiveness, sin appears as darkness, confusion, and mystification. Until evil is seen in the light of God's creation and redemption of the world, our abortive agonies and struggles are viewed as the very fabric of man's life and world, a view that excludes redemption and ends in bitter cynicism. Only within a Christian understanding of evil can life be accepted as good.

This mystery is sung with wonder in Orthodox hymnography, as the worshiper expresses his gratitude for the blessed effects of Christ's condescendence:

> What can we give back to the Lord for all that he gave us?
> For our sake he became man.
> For corrupted nature the Logos was made flesh and he
> dwelled within us, the benefactor for those ungrateful.
> For those who dwell in darkness he became the sun of justice.
> The impassible was brought to the cross,
> light to Hades,
> light instead of death, resurrection for the fallen.
> To whom let us raise our voice:
> Glory to Thee, O God.[86]

[86]Matins, Tone 7, sung during the Ainoi.

The Importance of Maintaining
the Dual Nature of Christ

THE INCARNATION of Christ entails a permanent presence in and impact on creation. What happened *ephapax* on Calvary is meant to continuously redeem history and humankind. Here lies the mystery of the divine-human nature of Christ and its effects upon anthropology in general. Without such a wide understanding of incarnation's effects, it remains impossible to overcome the opposition of history-transcendence, created-noncreated, eternal-temporal. Further results of the God-man relation can be seen in the role of Christians in a given culture in the world. Thus, one can see the importance of the doctrine of the two natures of Christ for the evolution of human history and of the mystery of the church for transforming human history.

In searching to solve the place of the gospel on earth, we sometimes underestimate its historicity for the profit of transcendence. The hidden danger, then, is to deny the presence of Christ in this world's events and to flee daily realities. It is a kind of escapism, a betrayal of our role. Or one may fall into the other extreme by rejecting the transcendence in order to save the daily events in life and history. In conformity to this, we then "desacralize" the gospel; we begin to preach a secularized God, identifying ideology and humanism with Christianity, and finally we arrive at a corresponding theology: "God is dead." In our days when all kinds of horizontal theologies of liberation through revolution flourish, patristics remind us that "humanization" is not an autonomous stream. Instead patristics help us maintain the balance of the spiritual with the material and, as in the hypostatic union of Christ's two natures, a theandrism. During the early christological conflicts, the Chalcedonian formula sorted matters out by rejecting both Nestorian dualism (separation of the divine-human realities in Christ), and Monophysitism (the belief that God has absorbed the human reality). This Council (451) stated that the divine and human are united in

Christ without confusion or division. The harmony of the two natures and two wills in Christ constitutes the foundation of the synergy of acts of God and of man.

Among others, Maximus the Confessor (662) defends christological theandrism. He discerns a synthesis within God's economy where the highest synergy operates between human and divine. He sees the whole secret of creation in the mystery of incarnation, thus manifesting the ontology of the created in its relationship to the uncreated. The synthesis of God and man in Christ explains not only the mystery of man itself but also the mystery of all creation. Nevertheless, all depends on man's attitude to Christ's offer, rejecting or accepting the possibility of becoming Christ-like. Defending the free human will of Christ against monoenergism, Maximus contributed to the correct development of the theandric notion. He was convinced that from the permanence of the human nature in Christ stems the truth of the permanent presence and communion with all those incorporated with him through baptism. In Christ the dependence of the human will on the divine will does not mean a passive submission. Otherwise it would deny human liberty and energy, and choose fatalism and quietism. This could also mean that humanity has nothing to do in the realm of salvation. Such a view would lead to another error, that God acts alone, excluding any reaction of his creatures. The fathers in general rejected the principle of passive submission to God without, nonetheless, falling into the opposite error of complete autonomy of the human element. A true union between God and man is based on a reciprocal action. God does not want his grace and truth to be received either by force or in a passive and blind way. He asks to be freely recognized as Lord. The casual creativity of God respects the principles of being and acting, which he has given to his creatures, and above all the free will of man.

In reality, divinization is the ontological innovation and the accomplishment of human nature in God. Human action and divine action interpenetrate in liberty. Such a metamorphosis of human nature is due to the uncreated energies of God, so familiar in the teaching of Simeon the New Theologian (1022), Gregory Palamas (1359), and Nicolas Cabasilas (1371). Let us say in this context that the imposition of supernatural grace on created grace is unknown in Orthodox theology.

Christ's divinity was never treated without reference to concrete consequences on human life. If the Nicene fathers fought so strongly against Arianism, against political oppression, and against so many other adversaries, the real reason was that the whole doctrine of Christian anthropology was at stake (and in real danger). That is why Christology is the nucleus of the teaching of Athanasius of Alexandria, whose preaching aimed at refuting the errors during the Arian crisis. The definition of the First Nicaean Council (325)— according to which Jesus is the Son of God, of the same substance as the Father, and true God issued from true God—constitutes the point of constant reference of its doctrine. Only if we accept this teaching are we entitled to speak of redemption, of salvation, of a real reestablishment of communion between man and God. Only the world of God redeems mankind perfectly. Without the incarnation man will remain in the state of his corrupted nature, from which nothing can liberate him, even a great number of sacrifices or penitential and expiatory actions.[87]

Liberated from corruption and the tragedy of the fall by Christ his Savior and Redeemer, and saved from the fear of death, man is reborn to a new life. He thus acquires again the true image of God, which has been deformed since his disobedience. He finds again his original beauty, his harmonious relationship with his Creator, broken since his exile from Paradise. St. Athanasius affirms: "The Word of God came down himself, in order that being himself, the image of the Father, he may again create man according to the image of God."[88]

Athanasius developed this theology of participation. Since God is communicative, man also becomes receptive of divinity—not necessarily of the divine nature, but of God's energies, of sonship, and of partaking of all of the heavenly Father's gifts. The first step is baptism in which man is freed from evil and transferred (transformed) to a new life—life with God. Sacramental life, inaugurated by baptism, makes available all blessings to the neophyte. The climax of this new life is centered in the classical expression "that the Logos of God is made man so that we all become divinized."[89] This *kaine*

[87]Athanasius, *De Incarnatione Verbi* (PG 25.144, 119).
[88]Ibid.
[89]Ibid.

ktisis articulates the reestablishment of what sin had destroyed: the knowledge of God and a radical change in man's behavior—moral as well as social.

In the light of the incarnation and of Christ's communion with us, we begin to learn something of what to do with suffering. Suffering's origin may be beyond finite knowledge but not its treatment. As always, we find the secret in our Lord's own life. He saw that if he continued on the course he had begun, the cross was unacceptable. Yet he welcomed it. And there are some, comparatively few in number and yet surely forming a vast multitude that no man can number, who learn from the Man of Sorrows and follow in his steps. For the joy that was set before him, Christ endured the cross. There are those who have begun to learn something of the secret of taking a bundle of thorns and twisting them into a glorious crown—of taking a cross, the gibbet of shame and disgrace, and transforming it into the means whereby a world of sinful men and women is drawn back to the loving arms of God.

We know that wherever we turn, Christ is suffering in the sufferings of his children. Such a spirit of sympathy should be ours too. The church fathers and all of the saints through the ages show in their writings the remarkable use which they have made of such enriching experiences. They are like the mountaineers who, having attained the summit, are able to see how all the ridges and gorges fit into the complete pattern; having taken part in the toil of climbing, they are all the more able to appreciate the efforts of each part of the climb, though their own horizons may be narrow and confined. For this is the manner of our grafting into Christ. We are incorporated in Christ by sharing his death and his victory over sin.

In the Gospel narrative, it is impossible to separate our call to believe in Christ from his call to live with him. Nor did Christ leave us with any misconceptions as to what this fellowship entails. The way of discipleship is the practice of the cross. It is as we bear in our bodies the dying of Christ that the life of the Lord will be manifested in us. All that he began is still going on. Yet he makes best use of those who show their loyalty by obedience. This may involve waiting. It may involve persecution. But the call to advance will come, and victory leads on to victory. Ascension speaks of victory. Christ reigns. He is on the throne. All through the Bible we notice that when the seers of God were in trouble they saw, never-theless, with the eyes of spiritual insight, a throne. Ezekiel in exile saw a throne. Daniel surveying "the abomination of desola-tion" saw a throne. John, a refugee on Patmos, saw a throne. In all of the darkness of their times, the martyrs saw a throne. This world is not ours. Nor does it belong to the evil powers of the Devil, al-though it seems like it does at times. It is God's world; Christ reigns. He has overcome the world. He assures all of his friends on the other side of death that there is a dear Mediator and Brother.

The Saving Action of
the Spirit

IMMEDIATELY AFTER the resurrection, the disciples began the mission entrusted to them by confessing the unity of the Triune God's action in the church. They particularly stressed the exceptional role of Christ, his crucifixion for the salvation of mankind. St. Paul affirms that the main object and the sole subject of his preaching is "Jesus Christ and him crucified" (1 Cor. 2:2). Before the creation of the world, God predestined us to be his adoptive sons so that our deification through Christ's sacrifice and sacraments takes place to the good pleasure of his Father's will, to the praise of the glory of his Spirit (see Eph. 1:4–6). For the Spirit of the Father is the epitome of wisdom and prudence; its grace reveals to us the Father's will and gathers into its harmony all things in heaven and earth. This Spirit will bestow upon godly people strength, endurance, and love so that they might respond to their calling.

The central place of Christ's death is seen in the essential part that the cross plays in Orthodox piety and liturgical life. The outward expression of being "crucified with Christ" is the too-often repeated sign of the cross, which is not only symbolical, but a real sign of one's own share in the crucifixion. By crossing ourselves "in the name of the Father, and of the Son, and of the Holy Ghost," we nail ourselves to the cross and insert ourselves in the church through the power of the crucified Lord. Ever since Christ's resurrection its salutary power acts invisibly in the world. This power is crowned by Christ's ascension—when the incarnate Son of God was seated at the right hand of the Father, thereby placing upon God's throne the deified human nature that had been accepted into his hypostasis—the sending of the Holy Spirit from the Father to bless the world.

Humanity, unable to reach God, was expecting a Savior. It was left to God to take the initiative of redemption, a theme treated so well by Cyril of Alexandria.[90]

[90]*Contra Julianum* I (PG 76.525).

It was impossible for man to attain that which surpassed his reason without the action of God who rules all things, who enlightens our reason, who pours forth wisdom, and who widens the range of our speech. This grace cannot, however, be granted indiscriminately to all but only to those who are beyond the fleshly passions, freed from earthly uncleanness, pure in mind, and familiar with the achievements of piety. It is to this end that the God of all, through the voice of David, says: "Be still, and know that I am God" (Ps. 46:10); and Christ says, "Blessed are the pure in heart, for they shall see God" (Matt. 5:8).

The living economy of the Spirit and its continuous outpouring of divine energy into the life of believers is seen throughout Orthodox ascetic spirituality and ecclesiastical hymnography. Any passive or inactive view of the Spirit in God's trinitarian economy is rejected by the patristics. John of Damascus states that "we share the Eucharist in order that the communicants may be united to the body of the Lord and his Spirit . . . The Lord's flesh is indeed life-giving Spirit, since it has been conceived from the *zoopoion pneuma*. That begotten of Spirit is also spirit [John 3:6]. I say all this without rejecting the life-giving and divine element."[91]

Not only are the eucharistic texts pneumatocentric, but they draw their strength from the Holy Spirit. The climax of the offering is exactly the descent of the Spirit in order to bestow upon the priest and, through the Eucharist, upon all the congregation, the blessings of the Spirit. The "communion of the Holy Spirit" is the clearest evidence and confirmation of the spiritual insight of the Liturgy, which finds its highest point in the *epiklēsis*. There is seldom one prayer in the church's services not invoking this communion with the Spirit. Basil of Caesarea clearly states, "The adorning of the church is explicitly and clearly performed through the Spirit."[92] From this principle, it ensues that the whole life of Christians is Spirit-centered—a fruit of the Spirit. Our life is not just morally beautiful, superior to others', intellectually elevated, and the like —some of the many vague and ambiguous terms used abundantly in humanistic modern language. Such words convey the Pauline "psychic" state (James 3:15). In contrast to this is the true "spiritual"

[91]*The Orthodox Faith* 4, 13.
[92]*De Spiritu Sancto* 39.

state. For the Spirit does not simply aim at correcting and improving our life, but at becoming our very life.

The eternal relationship of the Spirit to the Father and the Son is defined in the Creed by the following words: "who proceeds from the Father, and who is venerated and glorified together with the Father and the Son." Through this phrase, the fathers of the Second Ecumenical Council guaranteed and reconfirmed the divinity of the Spirit in the trinitarian economy. In other words,

> the Spirit is considered equal in honour and divine majesty to the other persons of the Trinity, and not to be subjected or viewed as inferior in the Trinity. He is an equal person, and as such, he acquires all the properties of the Father and of the Son. The Spirit is not begotten, nor does he proceed from the Son, but he is sent (*apostelletai kai didotai*) in time through the mediation of the Son."[93]

The Father, according to John of Damascus, has no beginning (*anaitios kai agennētos, ou gar ek tinos, ex eautou gar to einai exei*). He is self-existent, the very source and cause of the Godhead. The Spirit proceeds from the Father not by birth (*ou gennētos*) but by procession (*all' ekporeutōs*).[94] Of course, it is not easy to define the difference between a procession and a birth. Our restricted intelligence cannot seize the implications of this theological issue. Irenaeus, facing similar difficulties, blames those who want to scrutinize and understand the mystery of the Spirit through their poor rational abilities. He uses the example of a mosaic.

> A man owning a mosaic, representing the image of a king, takes apart the small pieces, breaking them into smaller ones, and tries to compose the figure of a dog or a fox. Finally, however, he asserts that the whole picture is royal since its constituent pieces are there. And those who are trying to use the same words and expressions in order to cover their errors behave in the same way.[95]

The supporters of the *Filioque* often refer to the infusion of the risen Christ, who said to his disciples: "Receive the Holy Spirit" (John 20:22). They conclude from this that the Spirit has as source and origin the Son of God. In reality, Christ wanted to show to his

[93]Athanasius of Alexandria, *Letter to Serapion* 1, 20 (PG 26.580).
[94]*The Orthodox Faith* 1, 8 (PG 94.821).
[95]*Against Heresies* 1, 8 (PG 7.521).

disciples by this symbolical infusion that during Pentecost they would receive the entire and complete Spirit sent by the Father while, at that moment, he offered a prefiguration of what would occur later. The Father, according to Athanasius, is the source; the Son is the river; and the Spirit is the water to be drunk.[96]

The Spirit is often described as the "life-giver" because he delivers us from chaos and provides all the necessary conditions for existence. This is why, as was already stated in the Old Testament, if God the Father were to withdraw his Spirit from the universe, every creature would cease to exist and every being would disappear from the earth:

> Thou hidest thy face, they are troubled: thou takest away their breath, they die, and return to their dust.
>
> Ps. 104:29, *KJV*

> If he set his heart upon man, if he gather unto himself his spirit and his breath . . .
>
> Job 34:14, *KJV*

Throughout the Old Testament, we see the Spirit constantly in action, working for the uplifting of man and for the maintenance of order in the universe.

[96]Athanasius of Alexandria, *Letter to Serapion* 1, 19 (PG 26.573).

Problems Behind the
Filioque *Clause*

MUCH ATTENTION was given in past and present discussions to the
Filioque clause. Its history is complicated. The clause did not exist
in the original text. The expression that the Holy Spirit proceeds
"from the Father and the Son" was developed by St. Augustine in
the early fifth century.[97] He describes the Holy Spirit as the "bond
of love" (*vinculum caritatis*) between the Father and the Son, and
so as "proceeding" from both. At the same time Augustine was
careful to point out that the Holy Spirit proceeds principally from
the Father, who remains the very source of Godhead. In 589, upon
the conversion of King Reccared from Arianism, the Council of
Toledo proclaimed the *Filioque*. Pope Leo III (795–816) refused
any change in the Creed. Two centuries later, in 1014, Pope Bene-
dict VIII made it official, thus helping to pave the way for the
rupture between East and West (1054). Later, some of the most
able theologians set out to defend the *Filioque* and its insertion
into the Creed: St. Anselm[98] and Thomas Aquinas.[99]

Recently in the West, a certain uneasiness about this issue has
developed, and many voices have been raised for the removal of
the *Filioque* clause. I think that in spite of its good effect such an
isolated step is not enough. What counts above all is that the whole
pneumatology should be restored; it should permeate the whole
structure of church life and spirituality. More room should be given
to the Third Person, the Holy Spirit, for the simple reason that the
Holy Spirit constitutes the entire institution of the body of Christ.
John Chrysostom says in this respect, "If the Spirit had not been
present, the church would not have been constituted. But as the
church is constituted, it is obvious that the Spirit is present."[100]
Independently of any different point to be stressed is the fact that

[97]Augustine, *De Trinitate* XV; XVII, 29.
[98]*De Processione Sancti Spiritus.*
[99]*Summa Theologiae* I, quaestio 36.
[100]Chrysostom, *In Sanctam Pentecosten,* Homily I, i, 3 (PG 50.459).

the Holy Spirit dwells permanently in the church and in the hearts of human beings as in a temple; the Spirit unceasingly sanctifies the church and leads it into all truth (John 16:13). Thus the gestures in favor of a return to the teaching of early Christianity must be completed and made coherent; otherwise, with a few isolated concessions, the lack of inner consistency and unity becomes evident.

Such reflections on the character of the Trinity would probably inevitably involve us in discussion with Islamic theology which, on the one hand, starts from the Koran statement, "God does not beget nor is he begotten" (II2.3). On the other hand, the Koran regards Mohammed as the Paraclete foretold by Jesus (61.5), referring thereby after all to a key statement of trinitarian tradition, John 16:7. Should argument turn here only on the meaning of the word "beget" and on the personality of the Holy Spirit rather than on the exact nature of the gospel to be proclaimed to every creature, and not only to particular nations or races?

In this last respect in particular, it is especially important for us to free ourselves from the widespread, cynical notion that atheism and agnosticism best correspond to the present world mentality. If we are to remain true to our missionary obligation in regard to that mentality, the first insight required is precisely that the Holy Spirit can free us from a regular flux of creativity and destruction by convincing our spirit that what opens out before it is eternal life in a new cosmos, not the limitlessness of "this world."

At this point, however, to say anything further would be to overstep our competence. Instead, let us allow one of the fathers of 381 to speak in the conviction that, beyond range of time and language, he says precisely what the Orthodox and non-Orthodox can only say jointly if they are to say anything at all on this matter:

> One concise proclamation of our teaching, an inscription intelligible to all, is that this people, which so sincerely worships the Trinity, would sooner sever anyone from this life than sever one of the three from the Godhead: of one mind, of equal zeal, and united to one another, to us and to the Trinity by unity of doctrine: that which is without beginning, and is the beginning, is one God.[101]

Methodius of Olympus (c. 311) underlined that through the participation of the Spirit we became as Christ (*oionei Christon*

[101]Gregory of Nazianzus, *Farewell Discourse to the Council Fathers.*

gegonoton tou piston kata metousian tou pneumatos).[102] Athanasius of Alexandria reminded the faithful of the centrality of the Spirit: "Without the Spirit we all are in danger of remaining foreigners and afar from God, but with the participation of the Spirit we become one with the Divinity."[103] Simeon, the New Theologian and Byzantine mystic (949–1022), sums up the effect of the life in the Spirit: "One cannot qualify a man of faith as perfect, if he has not received the Spirit of God, because only the gift of the most Holy Spirit enables us to become communicants and participants of God."[104]

All of these quotations from patristics show that the descent of the Spirit from the Father to the world becomes the life-giving spring, the source of inspiration, the divinizing means of overcoming our fragile nature, an operation so beautifully described by Cyril of Jerusalem.[105]

Thus the preeternal design of the Trinity for the salvation of man is realized in the church. After the incarnation of the Logos and the establishment of his mystical body, the church, the Trinity now has only one concern, to draw all to itself by granting salvation. The Father assures us that he does not desire the death of a sinner. The Son, sitting on the right hand of the Father, is incessantly interceding for us. And the Spirit intercedes for us with ineffable words. In Ignatius of Antioch's ecclesiology, we read that "the one body of Christ is above all else, the sign of his divinely beatific passion, as a passion of the Lord, truly born in the flesh of the house of David, crucified in the flesh under Pilate."[106] "With the cross in his suffering, Christ calls us to himself, as his members";[107] for to enter the church means to be made a disciple of him, who offered himself for us as an offering and a sacrifice to God (Eph. 5:2). Thence stems the new anthropology: Christians become stones in the temple of the Father, prepared in the economy of God the Father, raised on high by Christ's action, which is the cross, with the help of the Spirit.[108] Thus we are all fellow travelers—*theophoroi, naophoroi,*

[102]*Symposium* 8.
[103]*Contra Arianos* 3, 24.
[104]*Ethical Sermons* 10 and 4.
[105]*Catechetica* 16, 14, 19 and 17, 13 and 18, 23.
[106]*Letter to the Smyrnaeans* 1, 2.
[107]*Letter to the Trallians* 11, 2.
[108]*Letter to the Ephesians* 9.

christophoroi, hagiophoroi—that is, bearers of God, bearers of the temple, bearers of Christ, bearers of holiness, and in every way dominated by Christ's behests.

During the solemn vesper of the feast of Pentecost, the hymns and the prayers (while people kneel) are full of texts declaring the sanctifying power of the Spirit. At the same time, the close cooperation of the Trinity is shown. So at the vigil, in the *stichera,* we sing:

> Come, O ye people, let us worship the Godhead in three Persons, the Son in the Father with the Holy Spirit. For the Father, before time was, begat the Son, who is coeternal and is equally enthroned, and the Holy Spirit, who was in the Father, and was glorified together with the Son; one Might, one Essence, one Godhead. Adoring the same let us all say: O Holy God, who by the Son did make all things through the cooperation of the Holy Spirit: O Holy Mighty One, through whom we have known the Father, and through whom the Holy Spirit came into the world: O Holy Immortal One, Spirit of comfort, who proceedeth from the Father, and resteth in the Son: O Holy Trinity, glory to Thee.

Throughout the liturgical year, clergy and faithful ask on every occasion the help and succor of the same Spirit. The following hymn is characteristic of the richness and the disposability of the Spirit to be near us and to fill all human inadequacies:

> O heavenly King, Comforter, Spirit of Truth, present in all places and filling all things; Treasury of good things and Giver of life: Come, and take up thine abode in us, and cleanse us from every stain; and save our souls, O Good One.

Needless to say, in none of the prayers is the Spirit actually called "God," an indication of the influence of St. Basil's theology.

The Canon of the universal feast of the Exaltation of the Holy Cross (September 14), attributed to St. Cosmas, refers to the ineffable divine essence and action of the Trinity through the sanctifying and grace-bestowing feast. The hymnographer constructs an analogy using the number three.

> O ye children, equal in number to the Trinity, bless ye God the Father and Creator; sing ye the praises of the Word who descended and changed the fire to dew, and exalt ye above all for ever the most Holy Spirit, who gives life to all.

Another hymn, this one composed by St. Gregory of Sinai, says:

The Tree of Life and salvation,
the Tree of immortality,
the Tree of reason, the thrice-sweet Tree,
incorruptible and indestructible.
The threefold Cross, the honest Tree,
that carries in itself the Tri-hypostatic image
of the Trinity.

The ascetic fight of the faithful is steeped in direct communion with the life-giving Trinity, so beautifully expressed in the prayer by St. Joannicius the Great:

My hope is the Father,
my refuge the Son,
and my protection is the Holy Spirit—
Glory to Thee, O Holy Trinity.

In brief, Orthodox soteriology reveals the relation of the Trinity to the world in the following terms: the Father leads us to the Son; the Son leads us to the Spirit through his sacrifice once offered; the Spirit returns us to the Father. The whole mission of the church from the first day of Pentecost is activated by the Spirit. Thus there is a triune witness to creation in heaven: the Father, the Logos, and the Holy Spirit (see 1 John 5:7–8).

The incarnate Word enjoys an exceptional position in the economy of salvation. Through God's Word, the world was created, and without him was not anything made that was made (John 1:3). The Son of God accomplishes the restoration of the communion of the world with its Creator, which had been destroyed through man's fall. Christ is the focus and head of the church, which appeared in the world and acts in it as the true church of Christ. Without him nothing can be accomplished (John 15:5). He is the unique vine through which the divine lifeblood is restored in man.

Although God has nothing in common with the perishable created world insofar as its essence is concerned, he comes into contact with it through his economy or energy. God performs this function of "economy" beginning with the creation, and then by continuous and successive interventions. This explains why the Cappadocian fathers use the plurals "economies" and "energies."[109]

[109]See Chrysostom, *Homily* 4, 5 *on Genesis* (PG 53.44); *Homily* 34, 2 *on 1 Corinthians* (PG 61.287).

This action of God in the world does not involve any alteration in his divinity. In his dealings with the created world, God remains intact, beyond alteration. He keeps his distance from the vanities and corruptibility of human nature. The existing relationship between God and the world is not "in essence" (*kat' ousian*) but "in connection" (*kata schesin*). This relation is realized by God's presence in the world through his energies. Likewise, man participates in these energies of God, never having access in the divine essence which remains beyond sharing (*amethektos*). Thus John Chrysostom comments, "God has nothing in common with us; he has made himself a complete stranger to communion with the creation, and by communion I do not mean at all of the very essence of God but only that of relationship between him uncreated and eternally being and us created beings."[110]

As we well know, of all the many interventions of God in history for man's redemption, the major one was the incarnation. But as John Chrysostom points out:

> Even in this *enanthropisis* of the Logos, divinity united with humanity was not altered in its essence, because divinity has its own permanent, immutable, unaltered essence, excluding itself from any kind of change or influence. In Jesus Christ the incarnate Logos, there is a mysterious union of the two natures without confusion in these two natures. For the qualitative superiority of the divine element has assumed manhood as well, while the grandeur of the divinity has in no way been damaged. Let us use an analogy: when a king discusses a matter with a servant, he does not lose anything of his royal dignity because he has descended so low. On the contrary, it was sinful mankind which gained immeasurably from this *kenosis*, this condescendence of Christ. In this meeting of God and man, we do not have an entry of the human into the essence of divinity, as the pantheists claim, but only a participation in the divine energies. Christ is the Son of God in very nature and essence. Human beings, on the other hand, become sons of God by adoption, by grace (*kata charin*). For this reason Christ, while remaining the only begotten Son (the Monogenes) in the field of divinity, has many brothers (in the field of economy) enabling all to share with him and even to become coheirs of His kingdom.[111]

We see the same conditions regarding the action and economy of the Spirit. Its energies regarding mankind are many and multiform.

[110]Chrysostom, *Homily* 2, 4 *on John* (PG 59.34).
[111]Chrysostom, *Homily* 2, 1–2 *on St. John* (PG 59.79).

The Bible shows us this variety; it describes the Spirit as a dove, fire or water, and the like. All these names and symbolic illustrations relate not to the essence of the Spirit, since the essence is invisible and beyond reach and understanding, but to its energies. The bestowal of the Spirit does not lead to participation in the essence (*ousia*), but in its energies. The Paraclete remains indivisible in its essence but is divided in its energies. Through them the Spirit imparts to the body of man all the necessary conditions to become an instrument of virtue instead of earthly passions. Thus the Eucharist confirms its special character, being what Maximus the Confessor describes as a "Cosmic Liturgy."

But the Eucharist is not merely a framework of adoration and pious supplication. There exist many other, noneucharistic services for that purpose. Essentially, it is a call for intimate, divine communion through the *epiklēsis*. All the preparatory and ensuing stages are aimed in one unique direction: to entreat the Holy Spirit so that all the participants may become *pneumatophores*. As early in the ceremony as the Great Entrance, the celebrant says: "The Holy Spirit will himself celebrate with us all the days of our life." But the climax is seen at the actual moment of consecration of the offered elements of bread and wine, after the Words of Institution and the Anamnesis: "Send down your Spirit upon us and upon the gifts here present; bless them both, the bread and the chalice, by changing them through your Holy Spirit."

The Divine Liturgy at the same time plays an educational role: it confesses and teaches (*didaskein*). The reader of the consecratory texts is impressed by the wealth and precision of the doctrinal material presented, especially that of salvation economy and history. A teaching of exceptional quality is expounded about God, about Christ, and about the communion of saints. The two stages of Christ's incarnation, his hypostatic union without confusion, are expressed eloquently when the celebrant places the chalice and the bread on the altar separately:

> O Christ, bodily present in the tomb, spiritually present in the underworld, you, by virtue of your Godhead, were in Paradise with the good thief, seated upon the throne with the Father and the Spirit. You, the infinite One, who brings all things to fulfillment.

What is asked from the assembly is to open their hearts so that the "life-giving" Spirit may fill their innermost existence. It is the Holy Spirit who enables the *pleroma*, the church in general, to grasp all the elements of the mystery in their oneness, whether they be dogmas or spirituality. This is why the Orthodox Church knows no opposition between mysticism and theology, between personal experience of the sacraments and doctrine. Dogma expresses revealed truth, which comes to us in the guise of an unfathomable mystery. We ought to live it in such a way that, instead of assimilating the mystery to our manner of understanding, we have to undergo a deep change through it—an inward transformation that will make us ready for mystical experience.

The Oneness of the Church

WHAT ARE THE REASONS for formulating the article on the church: "I believe in one holy catholic and apostolic church . . . ?"

The answer is simple. After the exposition of God as the Lord of all, followed by the epiphany of Christ—who became as one of us for our salvation—and then pneumatology, the Nicene Creed wants to show that the saving action, the trinitarian economy, is worked out in the body of Christ. It links, therefore, soteriology and ecclesiology. Christ, as the head, is inconceivable without his body. Great damage has been done by the theological research of the last century stressing only the historical Jesus, isolating him from his people with whom he remains forever. An excessive ecclesiocentrism as well as an excessive Christomonism are equally unacceptable. Both are ruled out by the Nicene Creed. There we find a progressive, coherent order and a symmetry throughout the articles concerning the manifested actions of the Holy Trinity for the salvation of mankind and life everlasting.

The identification of the kingdom of God with the church in patristics bears significance for our subject. In a poetic form full of lyricism and analogies, Ephrem of Nisibis in Syria gives us a picture of the church as the love of God wanted it:

> He planted the garden most fair,
> and also built the church most pure.
> In the Tree of Knowledge
> He established the commandment.
> He gave joy freely—but they did not respond
> He gave a warning—but they were not sufficiently afraid.
> So in the church,
> God planted the Word,
> which gives joy by its promises
> and fear by its threats. . . .
> The Assembly of the Saints
> is a symbol of paradise.

Each day one can pick in it,
the fruit which gives life to all.
Here, my brothers, is pressed,
the fruit of the grape, the Medicine of Life.
When the blessed apostles
were gathered together,
then a quaking began.
It was like the fragrance of Paradise.
For Eden, knowing them as her guests,
gave generously of her fragrance.
Delight fell upon the apostles,
those heralds who were to instruct and to lead
the wedding guests to the banquet.
Eden, the friend of mankind, ran to welcome with joy,
all those who desired to enter.
Of your goodness, make me worthy,
to receive the gift of your Eden,
this treasure house of perfumes,
this store of fragrances.
For by its sweet-scented air,
I sate my hunger.
It is a fragrance which nourishes
each being of man for all his days.
Everyone who breathes it is gladdened with joy,
and forgets a need for bread.
This is the Table of God's kingdom:
Blessed is he who spread it in his paradise.[112]

In formulating the faith of the "one holy catholic and apostolic church," there is a strong conviction that the church cannot be many, but only one. How then can this unique one be distinguished from others?

Facing claims by the various heresiarchs to the effect that each represented the true church as desired by Christ, the ecumenical councils were forced to put an end to such arrogance by a clear statement. The church is not found wherever one wants. There are few distinctive signs guaranteeing its true identity such as those prescribed in the article: *una sancta catholica apostolica ecclesia*. Thus, any theory of relativist ecclesiology, which in our days is known as "branch theory," is utterly rejected. In fact, by introducing the principle of comprehensiveness, a churchly character is ex-

[112]Ephrem of Nisibis, *Hymns on the Paradise* VI, 7–8 and XI, 14–15.

tended to any religious body for the simple reason that it is a branch of the big tree of the church of Christ. So nobody can be discontent, and nobody can pretend to have the exclusive monopoly of ecclesiality.

The fathers, on the contrary, were extremely scrupulous in distinguishing the true church from pseudoecclesiastical groups. Facing a variety of Christian communities, each of which pretended to be the genuine one, they sought the authentic marks, the *notae ecclesiae*, which differentiated the church from schismatic bodies. Cyril of Jerusalem (386) faced this same difficulty in commenting on this article of faith. In his address to candidates for baptism (c. 348), he said that the term *ecclesia* could easily be used by anybody to make credible his own community. All the evildoers were using the same name—Marcionites, Manichees, and the like. Therefore, we are reminded not to give heed to them but to direct ourselves to the one catholic *ecclesia*. She is the mother of all of us, the spouse of Christ, the enduring *typos* of the celestial Jerusalem. Remaining within this unique church, we benefit from being taught properly and living uprightly, and thus we can gain the heavenly kingdom. It is named *ecclesia* because all are summoned up and gathered in, as it is said in Lev. 8:3: "and assemble all the congregation at the door of the tent of meeting." Cyril sees the sterility of the Jewish synagogue, the privileges having now passed over by means of Christ's incarnation to the holy church of Christians composed of the newly converted nations. Such an *ecclesia* was in the mind of St. Paul when writing to Timothy.[113] Cyril is sure about the safety of remaining within the boundaries of the *ecclesia*. He instructs the neophyte to live with the sheep and to avoid heretics as real wolves. He makes the plea, "Do not flee from the *ecclesia* . . ."[114]

Such considerations should be remembered in order to understand the patristic language when it praises with eulogies, metaphors, and analogies the church as the "ark of salvation." These considerations are reflected in the Pauline letter to the Ephesians, the longest treatise on the church found in the New Testament. The knowledge of being the chosen people of God gave a national identity to the Jews. But Paul states that those who trust in Christ antedate the

[113]See 1 Tim. 3:15; *Catechesis* 18, 22–28 (PG 33.1044–49).
[114]*Catechesis* 6, 35 (PG 33.601).

creation of the world, thus giving priority to the church even though the coming of Christ happened a long time after Israel was called (see Eph. 1:4-5).

This firm emphasis on the oneness of the church is relevant for recent debates. If the existing system of majority rule was applied to doctrinal issues, the Arians ought to have held the right faith because they were the prevailing group in those days and were spread throughout the empire. They even had the state with them, including eminent prelates and theologians. In fact, most provinces belonged to Arianism. Here one admires the attitude of the Emperor Theodosius. Without any hesitation, far from being a demagogue, he clearly sees on which side the Orthodox faith stands. Beyond the false numbers of statistics, he leans toward the minority of the Orthodox who are still maintaining a few strongholds. From this attitude, we learn that matters of faith cannot be judged by numerical size, by voting systems, or by counting ballots, as so often happens nowadays in ecumenical discussions.

The article on the church displays a mine of doctrinal wealth. As one can see, there is no teaching on man. This absence of anthropology is explained by the fact that for the Nicene fathers, man is not an isolated and autonomous being but is integrated into a fellowship of believers because of his baptism. He is an "ecclesial" being, thinking and living in community with others, in the *communio sanctorum*. In other words, the answer to anthropology is to be found in the ecclesiology which implies interdependence and sharing. Only there can one find the real relationship between God and man, and man with man. There is found the meeting place of our real existence, linked with our Creator and our brothers, relying on their *koinonia*, their solidarity, and on a common salvation. The church is not a society of scattered, saved beings who work for their salvation self-centeredly and separately, but all Christians are co-responsible, helping each other, offering prayers in communal worship, and sharing common tasks and destinies. The finality of man must be seen through the saving action of God in his divine-human church.

Christ's church brings us the knowledge of the Spirit; it permits us to become part of Christ's body. St. Paul emphasizes that Christians receive these blessings best in an "us" or in a community of believers, in the corporate body of the *ecclesia*. He views the church as an extension of Christ. We thank God for this membership because it is Christ's spouse, guided and directed by him to the salvation of our souls: "He has put all things under his feet and has made him the head over all things for the church, which is his body, the fullness of him who fills all in all" (Eph. 1:22–23).

Orthodox ecclesiology is based on the concept that a local assembly gathered in the name of Christ and headed by a bishop who celebrates the Eucharist is the focus and expression of catholicity. As every part of the eucharistic bread is the true body of Christ, so every local church is truly the catholic *ecclesia*. "Wherever Christ is, there is the catholic church," stated Ignatius of Antioch.[115] Church history begins with ecclesiastical units, scattered all over the world—the *oikumene*. The oneness of the church in every given locality is the first concrete embodiment of that unity which forms the nature of the church; it is the unity of believers regenerated into new life by Christ, who have "one Lord, one faith, one baptism" (Eph. 4:5). To the divisions of the world, the church counterposes the unity in God which surpasses all racial, national, linguistic, or social differences. For the early Christians, the unity of the church was a fact and not a mere dogmatic definition with no outward expression in life. Whatever the increase of local communities, the unity of the church remained inviolable because in all communities there was the one and the same eucharistic synaxis *united and uniting*.

Irenaeus of Lyons expounds as follows the catholicity of the universal church:

> The church, although scattered throughout the whole world even to the ends of the earth, has received the faith from the apostles and from their disciples . . . Since the church has received the preaching and this faith although she is scattered, she preserves it carefully as one household. The whole church alike believes in these things, as having one (soul) and (heart), and in unison preaching these beliefs, teaches and hands them on as having one mouth . . . For though there are many different languages in the world, still the meaning of the tradition is one and the same. And there are no different beliefs or traditions in the churches established in Germany, or in Spain, or among the Celts, or in the East, or in Egypt or Libya, or those established in the center of the earth. But just as the sun, God's creature, is one and the same in all the world, so the preaching

[115]*Ad Smyrnaeos* 8, 2.

of the truth shines everywhere and enlightens all men who wish to come to the knowledge of the Truth.[116]

The oneness of the church is identified by the *Didache* with the Eucharist, because it is the sacrament of unity which gathers local communities from the ends of the world into the one catholic *ecclesia*: "As this broken bread was scattered upon the mountains and was gathered together and became one, so let thy church be gathered together from the ends of the earth unto thy kingdom."[117]

Ignatius of Antioch, one of the earliest postapostolic writers, sees the body of believers not as an abstract or amorphous reality but as a concrete community around the presbyter, the bishop, and the people, centered in the love of Jesus Christ. All live in harmony through and after the council of the apostles and the deacons, having had the ministry of Christ entrusted to them.

Here are two important classical extracts closely related to our subject:

Now concerning my fellow servant, Burrhus, your deacon by the will of God, who is blessed in all things, I beg that he may stay longer, for your honor and for that of the bishop. And Crocus also, who is worthy of God and of you, whom I received as an example of your love, has relieved me in every way—may the Father of Jesus Christ refresh him in like manner—together with Onesimus and Burrhus and Euplus and Fronto, in whose persons I have seen you all in love. May I ever have joy of you, if I be but worthy. It is, therefore, seemly in every way to glorify Jesus Christ, who has glorified you, that you may be joined together in one subjection, subject to the bishop and to the presbytery, and may in all things be sanctified.

Seek, then, to come together more frequently to give thanks and glory to God. For when you gather together frequently the powers of Satan are destroyed, and his mischief is brought to nothing, by the concord of your faith. There is nothing better than peace, by which every war in heaven and on earth is abolished.

It is better to be silent and be real, than to talk and to be unreal. Teaching is good, if the teacher does what he says. There is then one teacher who "spoke and it came to pass" and what he has done even in silence is worthy of the Father.

He who has the word of Jesus for a true possession can also hear his silence, that he may be perfect, that he may act through his speech, and be understood through his silence. Nothing is hidden from the

[116]*Against Heresies* I, 10, 1–2.
[117]*Didache* 10, 5.

Lord, but even our secret things are near him. Let us therefore do all things as though he were dwelling in us, that we may be his temples and that he may be our God in us. This indeed is so and will appear clearly before our face by the love which we justly have to him.

If Jesus Christ permit me through your prayers, and it be his will, in the second book, which I propose to write to you, I will show you the dispensation of the new man Jesus Christ, which I have begun to discuss, dealing with his faith and his love, his suffering and his resurrection; especially if the Lord reveal to me that you all severally join in the common meeting in grace from his name, in one faith and in Jesus Christ, "who was of the family of David according to the flesh," the Son of Man and the Son of God, so that you obey the bishop and the presbytery with an undisturbed mind, breaking one bread, which is the medicine of immortality, the antidote that we should not die, but live forever in Jesus Christ.[118]

Knowing the great orderliness of your love toward God I gladly determined to address you in the faith of Jesus Christ. For being counted worthy to bear a most godly name I sing the praise of the churches in the bonds which I carry about and pray that in them there may be a union of the flesh and spirit of Jesus Christ, who is our everlasting life, a union of faith and love, to which is nothing preferable, and (what is more than all) a union of Jesus and the Father. If we endure in him all the evil treatment of the Prince of this world and escape, we shall attain unto God.

Forasmuch then as I was permitted to see you in the person of Damas, your godly bishop, and the worthy presbyters Bassus and Apollonius, and my fellow servant the deacon Zotion, I would enjoy his friendship because he is subject to the bishop as to the grace of God, and to the presbytery as to the law of Jesus Christ.

Seeing then that there is an end to all, that the choice is between two things, death and life, and that each is to go to his own place; just as there are two coinages, the one of God, the other of the world, and each has its own stamp impressed on it, so the unbelievers bear the stamp of this world, and the believers the stamp of God the Father in love through Jesus Christ, and unless we willingly choose to die through him in his passion, his life is not in us.

Seeing then that I have looked on the whole congregation in faith in the persons mentioned above, and have embraced them, I exhort you: Be zealous to do all things in harmony with God, with the bishop having the primacy after the model of God, and the priests after the model of the council of the apostles, and the deacons (who are so dear to me) having entrusted to them the ministry of Jesus

[118]Ignatius of Antioch, *Letter to the Ephesians* 2, 13, 15, 20.

Christ—who from eternity was with the Father and at last appeared to us.[119]

The dichotomy undertaken by the Reformation between the Scriptures and the *didaskalia* in the church creates a certain skepticism; the latter is nothing if not the doctrinal tradition. Of course, it is dangerous to identify Scripture and *didaskalia*. But it is also perilous to separate them completely, as if they were contradictory. Their fullness lies in the fact that they constitute one indivisible living truth. As the Scriptures, so also the dogmas are living in the liturgical life of the church with only this difference: while the Holy Bible remains a corpus determined and fixed forever, excluding any possibility of reduction or addition, the tradition of dogmas, although stable, is subject to reformulation and analytical application where and when needed. The church can express in new terms and more acceptable language the revealed truth. This does not mean that the doctrines are fluid and in a continuous process of formulation. At every historical moment, the church can formulate our Christian faith in appropriate dogmas, reflecting the substance of truth as revealed in Scripture.

Moreover, limiting the revelation exclusively to written forms displays an ignorance of Christ's incarnation, whereby the invisible became visible. God manifests his truth through channels corresponding to human nature, as both spiritual and material. Consequently, a good deal of the teaching of the divine is known in a "hylomorphic" way. If a certain amount of doctrine is to be found in the Bible par excellence, on account of the limitations of human intelligence, an equal amount of Christ's *didaskalia* is articulated through sacraments. Sacraments are complementary, helping us to know what an invisible doctrine cannot convey.

We know how often the fathers used the term "image" in order to develop Christology: the Son of God is the image of the Father. There is a similitude of the Father with the Son, although each Person constitutes a particular hypostasis. In the same way, all liturgical signs, customs, icons, rites, and the like are images of saving truths: they reflect and convey what they represent. What the word is unable to tell is translated into symbol and lived liturgically. One element complements the other. The church teaches the redeeming truths in a synthetic way using both expressions, the re-

[119]Ignatius of Antioch, *Letter to the Magnesians* 1, 2, 5, 6.

vealed truth as is found in the Bible and also its continuity and historicity in the life of the church, according to the divine-human nature of this truth.

Maximus the Confessor sees on each Christian the very reflection of what he believes—its essence, namely, that all marks of the Christian faith are manifested in his personal life: "If man is a microcosm, then subsequently, the church is a macro-anthropos."[120] Thus must be understood why this church, the assembled, redeemed people of God, has had an astonishing impact on humanity. It has had this impact precisely because it communicates the saving grace of God. What they all together do in a communal way, each also does separately and personally as an ecclesial being. By the cosmic extension and witness of the Eucharist, the saints, as human persons living in space and time, become the hypostasis of a new humanity in the process of being transfigured, transformed, renewed, and built up from the ruins of the fallen world to create the kingdom of God. History, therefore, is nothing else than the field of continuous divinizing action of the synaxis and of each person as well, separately.

[120]*Capita theologica* I, 73 (PG 90.1209a).

Conciliarity

CATHOLICITY AND APOSTOLICITY meet at a council. Thus the unity of the church is confirmed and maintained even among scattered local communities. The church, a "synod in permanent session," continues to be constituted as such by the Holy Spirit of God. The overall consensus or symphony of the church reaches its culminating point in the ecumenical councils. These are the perfect expression of the prevailing spirit of collegiality among the autocephalous churches. As such, they have proved themselves to be the highest authority in the church. In particular, the ecumenical councils act as the supreme ecclesiastical body for formulating the faith of the church and ratifying for all times and places the church's common voice regarding worship, order, and discipline. At the same time they condemn emerging errors and work for the preservation of church unity, enshrined in doctrinal unity. They have spoken with divine authority chiefly on matters of faith in the Holy Spirit. It is just this which the fathers who took part in them expressed in the apostolic formula, "It has seemed good to the Holy Spirit and to us" (Acts 15:28), thereby copying the example of the apostles.

The close relation between apostolic preaching and the faith of the church guarantees the divine origin of the church and the importance of the ecumenical council as the visible manifestation of this faithfulness. That is why Cyril of Alexandria states, with regard to the fathers of the Nicene Council, "It was not at all they who were speaking, but the Spirit even of God the Father."[121] In this context, one must not confuse rigidity of formulation with doctrinal exactness. Never has the church identified exterior form with substance. If time dictates it, the church can complete, reinterpret, reformulate, and perfect a given doctrine. The patristic church was always reluctant to provide dogmatic definitions, these being a specific feature of Western thinking. The conciliar practice appears

[121]*Letter* 39 (PG 77.181).

very early, right at the end of the apostolic period. It is noteworthy that during the anti-Arian era, the Orthodox did not use juridical terms to justify the authority of the Council of Nicaea; instead, they used the fact of its wide representativity[122] as a guarantee of the catholicity of the accepted resolutions.[123]

Being the expression of the conscience of the universal church, a council was superior to any of the sees of the empire and even to the apostolic sees. Thus every time that the ratification of the honorary status of the bishop of Rome was sought, it did not constitute a superior authority over the council itself but simply allowed the whole Western world through its ecclesiastical head to adhere to the conciliar decisions. As an example, the case of Honorius, the pope condemned by the Sixth Council, shows that a conciliar body possessed the authority to condemn even a pope. Both the irrevocability and the authority of a council were so deeply ingrained in the conscience of the church that its decisions were considered to be the voice of God. Thus the Emperor Constantine, writing to the Alexandrians concerning the status of the First Council, states:

> That which has commended itself to three hundred bishops cannot be other than the judgment of God; the Holy Spirit dwelling in the midst of men endowed with such character and dignity has brought to light the will of God.[124]

In the early church, the church itself was not the subject of abstract reasoning or even disputes. She was the living reality of all theology. From the days of Ignatius of Antioch, the term "catholic" was identical with the true body of Christ on earth; consequently, the word "catholic" was later included in the Nicene-Constantinopolitan Creed. The concept of this term emphasizes the unity of the living communities of believers—the gathering of all into oneness—who express the one faith in one voice. This meaning of catholicity in relation to conciliarity is explained thoroughly by Cyril of Jerusalem:

> The church is called "catholic" because it extends through all the world, from one end of the earth to another. Also because it teaches

---

[122]Athanasius, *Epistula ad Afros episcopos* 2 (PG 26.1032).

[123]With regard to the Chalcedonian injunction "neither to add or subtract from the Creed" is meant the substance of the dogmas but not the language, when necessary, and any reformulation for pastoral needs if it was imposed.

[124]Socrates, *Church History* I, 9 (PG 67.85).

universally and without omission all the doctrines which ought to
come to man's knowledge . . . and because it brings under the sway
of true *religion all classes* of men . . . and because it universally
treats and cures every type of sin, committed by means of soul and
body, and possesses in itself every kind of virtue which can be
named, in deeds and words, and spiritual gifts of every kind.[125]

We have unreservedly to view this Council of 381 as a significant
event in the history of the church and of dogma. We hear Gregory
of Nazianzus's farewell discourse to the Council where he speaks of
the place of their conciliar victory. In an autobiographical poem, he
recalls how that victory long hung in the balance—on a knife-edge.
The main task of this Council was to hold fast to what the Nicaean
fathers had established in order to crush Arianism and to add solely
what had not yet been made sufficiently clear, namely, the divinity
of the Spirit.

Furthermore, we realize that something more was accomplished
here than a mere recapitulation. Since Constantine's death, church
and empire had changed too much, the former scarcely to its advantage. Orthodoxy opened up for Theodosius a vista which neither
a local cult (whether Christian or non-Christian) nor a church
group could offer. The fathers of this Council were detached in
their attitudes toward the centers of political power—more so than,
for instance, Eusebius of Caesarea or Ambrose and Damasus,
Eusebius's Western contemporaries. Even when the fathers engaged
in matters of church policy, as did Basil of Caesarea and, to some
extent, Gregory of Nazianzus, they came less into conflict with the
emperor than with rival church groups, especially with the anti-
Western attitudes of the Greek and oriental bishoprics.

If Gregory of Nazianzus criticized this Council, he did so not because he regarded its Creed as an intolerable compromise, but because he considered the increasingly rival self-consciousness of the
West and, above all, of the East in the church of his time to amount
to denial of a dogma, the content of which is none other than an
economy of salvation which, far more than all forms of universalism
since Hellenism, opens up a perspective in which all world religions
fall within a single historical horizon. The outcome of the Creed is
a definition of the content of catholicity and the profession of faith

[125]*Catecheses* 18, 23.

in a salvation which is coextensive with all epochs of history: I believe in "one baptism for the forgiveness of sins . . ."

It is indeed sad that Christians often lose sight of and betray the new life which they have received as a gift through their baptism. We live and act as if Christ had never hung three long and agonizing hours on the cross, as if he had never died that we might have life, as if he had never risen from the dead. Our daily cares and preoccupations cause us to forget, and because we forget, we fail. The Liturgy becomes too long for us, so we must shorten it. Fasting and penitential acts become difficult and irksome, so they must be minimized or, better still, done away with. And so on, ad infinitum. Because of our failure, life again becomes "old," petty, dark, and meaningless. We become drifters on a meaningless journey with no object in sight, no goal to reach. In our self-pity we virtually succeed in forgetting death itself; but it is still there, omnipresent. Someday in the midst of our high living and worldly enjoyment, it will come upon us sudden and horrible, real and inescapable. The great tragedy of nominal Christianity is that we do not attach our lives to Christ because we are taken up with the cares and pleasures of the world.

If we are cognizant of this fact, then we may and can truly understand what liturgical life penetrated by the resurrection really is, and why it needs and presupposes a catharsis and *metanoia*, a time of preparation. If we recognize our failure and shortcomings, then fasting and acts of penance have meaning for us and their value is understood. The liturgical traditions of the church too, with all the various cycles and services, have meaning and value when we understand that they exist in order to help us recover the vision of the new life which we so easily lose and so often betray. It is the church, ancient in her traditions and wise in her knowledge of things divine, which reveals to us things which "no eye has seen, nor ear heard, nor the heart of man conceived," but which "God has prepared for those who love him." The church, which is in this world but not of this world, teaches us by her rich liturgical life at the center of which is the Paschal Lamb, the resurrected Christ. The entire worship of the church is organized around the Feast of the Resurrection. The liturgical year with its seasons and feasts becomes a journey, a pilgrimage, toward its goal—the Pascha, the

Omega, which at the same time is the Alpha, the end of all that
which is old and the beginning of that which is new—a steady and
constant pilgrimage of "passover" from "this world" into the "kingdom" revealed to us in Christ.

To theologize is to participate in the new creation. Baptism is the
beginning, the first point, the first fruits of theology and of the
vision of God. True theology is in the gift of God to man in Christ
and, therefore, in the church. It is a total reality which embraces
the whole man and the whole world because it sets the world on a
new basis, which integrates it and restores it to its integrity and true
order.

In recent years, there has appeared a sexist movement of equality
determined to reformulate the fatherhood of God in a "bisexual
way," as they say. The object of this movement is to show the injustice of a "patriarchal" God, proposing instead a God both Father
and Mother, so that there is no sexual discrimination. The worst
distortion, however, has taken place in ecclesiology. The unicity of
the church as one holy catholic and apostolic is contested. Every
gathering of the baptized, under the pretext of being faithful to the
Bible and assembled in his name, wants to acquire the same title
as if it constituted a church regardless of whether it has all the distinctive ecclesiastical marks to give it credibility. The attribute
"catholic" has long been the subject of abuse by the Church of
Rome, restricting its meaning to the Western Roman communion.
Further, the unity issue has become so negotiable, so easily manipu-
lated, so compromising, so anemic and flexible, that each denomina-
tion stresses one single aspect of it, thinking it to suffice for recognition as fulfilling all the requirements of the one church that Christ
wanted.

Even worse is the trend by post-Reformation Free Churches
toward relativizing certain indispensable marks of the oneness—tradition, ministry, episcopacy, apostolic succession accompanied by
apostolic faithfulness, eucharistic structure, sacraments, conciliarity,
and collegiality—and replacing the true mission of the church in a
rather selective domain with all kinds of commitments in the socio-
political field. This has taken place to such an extent that the church
is losing its authentic aspect, becoming instead an ideology, a
humanistic institution with excellent ideals, another edition of the
Red Cross. We are facing a confusion of ecclesial understanding

and social solidarity. For God's sake, not underestimating human needs, we want to underline the great hidden danger that Christ's church in healing human evils will confine itself to treating external symptoms. Rather, it must make a thorough diagnosis and attack real causes: selfishness, pride, absence of a genuine relationship between man and God and between man and man—with the vertical and horizontal, the divine and the human, brought together.

Today in the ecumenical movement we meet this tragic parody in our disunity. We confess the same Creed whilst holding diametrically opposite views. Our surprise grows as we see that the anniversary of the Creed was met by a certain apathy and a lack of awareness instead of a return to our common sources and to self-criticism for a real confrontation with the challenging Creed. Are we afraid of changing the status quo? We cannot escape a timely and challenging question addressed to all of us: if the Nicene fathers were present today among us in such a divided and subdivided Christianity, which one of the many churches would recognize itself as one holy catholic and apostolic? It is not logical to rely upon such a simplistic, naive, and widespread panacea as relativistic ecclesiology—that is, "that the church is here and at the same time is there, everywhere; we are all branches of the same tree" and that consequently nobody can pretend to have an exclusive monopoly on this oneness of the *Una Sancta*. Where can this one church be found? This is a challenging, salutary question for all Christians today.

Let us not put forward as an argument for the authenticity of the professed faith the numeric factor, that is, the majority or minority of public opinion. Statistics have little to do in the field of error or orthodoxy. In many dark pages of church history the true faith was maintained by a small number of believers while the majority was in the hands of heretics, as in the case of Arianism. Nor let us misuse the ultra-institutionalism of the Holy Spirit, referring to the New Testament text that "it blows where it wills." If such were literally the case, then anarchy and confusion would have long since resulted. The fathers taught that the unity of the church proceeds from the one Lord, the one Spirit, and is based on the *symphonia* of doctrine among the members of the ecclesiastical body. It cannot be otherwise since heterogenous views cannot cohabit; this would contradict the very meaning of the oneness of the body of Christ, the church, as an assembly of those who are one, who hold the same faith.

Basil of Caesarea says, "One is the holy yard of those who are one in God."[126] John Chrysostom says, "This very name of the *ecclesia* is a name implying concord and symphony."[127] Elsewhere Chrysostom says, "The church was instituted by Christ, not that we the assembled might be divided, but that those divided might become reconciled."[128]

We appreciate the efforts of many Reformed bodies to find what they call "confessional identity," inasmuch as certain traditional positions are not accepted theologically by all. But in seeking this identity, they tend to exaggerate the authority of their respective "confessional" texts while also trying to indicate that they agree with the ancient creedal texts. Thus they risk falling into the trap of "confessionalism," that is, putting an accidental relative document of history which concerns one particular body on a par with the faith of the undivided church, enjoying the consensus of all the churches and so having as its credentials catholicity, continuity, and permanency. Any new, heterodox doctrine, however, risks making matters more complicated and certainly does not facilitate the object of unity for which we are all striving.

The Bible, with all of Yahweh's theophanies, is read by the fathers in the light of Christ's incarnation and the redeeming mission of the church. A marvelous synthesis is thus achieved, revealing a wise soteriological plan worked out by the same God in the history of salvation. Patristics look to the whole truth of saving divine action in all its dimensions according to the need for universality or "catholicity." Gregory of Nyssa illustrates this:

> The great Paul was such a river of perfumes flowing from the garden of the church through the Spirit, whose streamlet was Christ's fragrance; and other such rivers were John and Luke, Matthew and Mark, and all the others, the noble plants in the garden of the bride, who were moved by that luminous southern wind to become sources of perfume, shedding forth the fragrance of the Gospels.[129]

[126]*Commentary on the Psalms* 28, 3 (PG 29.288); see also *Commentary on Isaiah* 5, 172 (PG 30.405).
[127]*Commentary on Galatians* 3 (PG 61.646).
[128]*Sermons on Corinthians* 27, 3 (PG 61.228).
[129]*On the Song of Songs,* Oration 10 (PG 44.985).

As we see, all the books of the Bible are used typologically to explain Christology and ecclesiology—a remarkable chorus, each complementing the other, offering a symphonia. The reflections of Solomon, the lamentations of Jeremiah, the pathetic cries of the psalmist, and above all the incomparable visions of Moses are evoked as anticipatory of the words of Jesus and his disciples. For Gregory of Nyssa, for example, the trinitarian dogma is traced clearly and as early as the first pages of the Old Testament:

> It is the light of theology which shines through it, as through a window. Gen. 1:26 does not say "make man" in the singular, but "let us make man." It says so that you may understand the sovereignty, that is, that you may not ignore the Son in knowing the Father; also that you may understand that the Father created through the Son and the Son created with the Father's will; and thus, you may glorify Father in Son, and Son in Holy Spirit.
>
> So you are a common work in order that you may also become a common worshiper of both, not tearing apart the worship, but uniting the Godhead. See a narrative in form, but theology in power.[130]

Thus, the Old Testament could not be properly read outside of the living context of the church. Theology is the theology of the church and in the church.

[130]*Making of Man* (PG 44.260c).

Living the Mystery of
the Church

WHAT HAPPENS TO the Christian through his membership in the church is a mystery. The moment he joins the church he acquires all the qualities of the church. Thus he becomes holy in the same way that the church is holy. He becomes both a visible and a hidden mystery in the same way that the church is a hidden and a visible mystery. For we cannot explain the very substance of the body of Christ. It longs to be like its master, Christ. In the same way, the Christian lives because of the church, and as a member, he is nourished by its wholesome liturgical origins. This nourishment is provided in a visible and an invisible form. But the effects are clear because the conduct and behavior of a true Christian make him stand out from others. He lives the mystery in all its dimensions. He lives like others in the world, but he lives differently.

He lives against the flow, against the heart, against history. He is not a man who compromises with the world. He does not follow; he resists. Sometimes he will refuse to the point of accepting martyrdom rather than contradict his conscience. He receives the sacraments so that he himself becomes a sacrament, a mystery, by his life and through his testimony. "He identifies with that he receives," said St. Augustine. In other words, to live the mystery of the church means conforming to the characteristics, the properties (*idiomata*) of the church. He becomes a microcosm of the church not because he is without sin, but because he struggles constantly against sin. And if he falls, he can take advantage of the means available for regaining his health and restoring the love of God.

In what now follows we will try to describe the relation between the faithful and the church where, unmistakably, we find that this mystery is lived not esoterically, but in a real and tangible manner.

The initial link with Christ, the inaugurating Sacrament of Baptism, incorporates one at the same time into both him and his brethren. From now on the head and body together constitute a complete wholeness, both human and divine, earthly and heavenly in its character. How can one live this reality? Of course such a life is and will remain a mystery. Nevertheless, we can touch on certain distinctive elements which differentiate other concepts from that of the Orthodox ecclesiology of belonging. Such a theme acquires topicality in view of our dialogue with other Christians.

Living the reality of membership in Christ's church is vital for the church. The corporate aspect has an important repercussion upon a Christian's character, the way he feels and sees people as well as the things around and within himself. It was to such a community of redeemed people, in spite of human weakness and imperfections, that Christ was referring when he guaranteed the unconquerable nature of the church, that is, that no power of Hades would prevail over her (Matt. 16:18). Repeatedly Christ promised that he would sustain his body by bestowing graces or charismata. The dialectic between human and divine factors, as often distinguished by the reformers, seems artificial. The one does not preclude the other. Throughout the history of salvation, God has used man's power, ability, and cooperation synergistically for his divine plan—his economy.

When formulating the order of the Christian faith, the fathers of the Second Ecumenical Council of Nicaea found nothing wrong with putting "faith in God," "faith in Christ," and "faith in the church" side by side. The records of the Book of Acts are centered on the church's reality in history, its saving, evangelizing, and growing through the apostles. Nobody relied on a closed, self-centered individual or on an inner witness of the Holy Spirit. Christians lived this reality in an ecclesial way, with their pastors and their community and not by themselves. The absolute criterion for verifying the gospel's sayings was not a person's own view, but that of the whole *pleroma* of the assembled faithful, the *ecclesia*. The Bible was read before the whole Christian assembly and understood by the church as a whole. "*Securus judicat orbis terrarum*," wrote St. Augustine, and this security has supported Christians through the centuries.

Faith in the mystical body of Christ, the church, is a reality that surpasses human understanding. The ninth article of the Nicene Creed expresses this by describing the church as "one holy catholic and apostolic." Of course, faith in the church is not a substitute for faith in God. To believe in the church is to believe that it is the mystical fountain of grace on earth, the abode of the grace of God throughout all ages where man receives sanctification (Matt. 16:18; Eph. 3:21). To have faith in the church means to venerate the communion of Christ and his people. It is through the church that man can rightly know the unity of God in the Trinity. The church is the image of this trinitarian oneness. As a member of the church one can apprehend, through spiritual striving, something of the ineffable divine essence and redeeming action of the Holy Spirit within the church.

Being the body of Christ, the living symbol of Christ's incarnation, the church is fully in possession of all that is required for man's sanctification. In other words, faith in Christ leads us to the church. Life in Christ is life in the church. Thus he who does not believe in the church is unable to understand the fullness of Christ's incarnation. The words of St. Paul apply only to those who believe and abide in the church: "You are no longer strangers and sojourners, but you are fellow citizens with the saints and members of the household of God, built upon the foundation of the apostles and prophets, Christ Jesus himself being the cornerstone, in whom the whole structure is joined together and grows into a holy temple in the Lord; in whom you also are built into it for a dwelling place of God in the Spirit" (Eph. 2:19–22).

Thanks to the hypostatic union of divine-human natures, it became possible for the church to act against any self-affirmation or apotheosis of man. Thus is refuted the pessimistic transcendentalism of a certain Protestant anthropology, manifested especially in the claim that original sin had destroyed in man even the image of God, and equally a purely humanistic "immanentism" which ignores the relationship between the divine and human in Christ. After all, both of these tendencies lead to secularism. One of the methodological difficulties for Westerners in understanding the patristic soteriology is that the fathers never isolate or dichotomize in fragments, but their outlook is holistic or "catholic." The fathers synthesize, treating man as a whole, composite being; they avoid divisions and oppositions where realities mutually complete one another. Historical-transcendent, celestial-earthly, body-spirit, temporal-eternal, human-God— all of these realities coexist without one excluding the other. Although humankind is destined for eternity, this eternity is not absolutely a future *eschaton* or far-distant event for the simple reason that man lives this future already now. Time and space contain something of the after-death reality. Man participates in God's life here and now. *Theōsis* begins now, although its fulfillment will be obtained in the life to come. God's glory is seen in those pious people who already live for him, animated for the divine *eros*.[131]

The theological crisis in the West is not as critics complain, that is, that the church is not present in human realities, but is indifferent to tragedy, injustices, and oppression. Nor is the crisis that theology is unable to speak a contemporary language to the man in the street. Rather, the theological crisis is that the church has not rendered to frustrated humanity the true image of the lordship and love of God, the Pantocrator and Savior, with his *philanthropia* intervening in history in order to liberate man from the tyranny of his self. Only thus can we see the issues of insecurity and fear and the perils of an autonomous view of man revolting against God. God's presence is not against man's freedom and happiness; on the contrary, God's presence is for man's promotion in the fullest sense. God did not want to abandon man after the fall. His love alone can explain his initiatives throughout history to help mankind, to reveal truth and liberate from error. In doing so, God never acts alone but relies upon man's consent, his *synergia* with God.

John of Damascus (675–749) in *De Fide Orthodoxa* recapitulated the whole problem of Christ's humanity and the saving aspects of Christology. In his comprehensive presentation of the teaching of the Greek fathers, he develops more than others the conception of *perichoresis* (*circumincessio*) in order to express intertrinitarian relations. He finds the end of this synthesis of Greek theological thought in the restoration of fallen man to his former state. He teaches that in the hypostatic union the Logos served as "hypostasis" —Person—to the humanity which he took. Hence he adopted the *enypostasia* of Leontius of Byzantium, which he interprets along the lines of the *communicatio idiomatum*. He sees in the interpenetration of the two natures in Christ the formation of theandric activities.

Man cannot be saved by himself. He needs a *christosoteria*. Christ's mission was not to offer simple, excellent moral precepts

[131]See Gregory of Nyssa, *Epistulae* (PG 37.1327).

but to save man from the bondage of fallen nature, to enable him to reach God's height, and to inherit with him all the blessings. From Old Testament times on, the entire divine economy aimed at helping man toward this direction of restoration. We must read more and more from the patristic texts concerning Christ's redeeming action and their repercussion on man's struggle for liberation and humanization.

The possibility of a reunification of the fallen creature and knowledge is realized in the person of Christ, the second Adam. In his Person was incorporated the whole human race: *anakephalaiosis*. Through the first Adam, human nature was deprived of the possibility of communion with the divinity. In the process of historical events, this impossibility was felt more strongly than participation (*metochē*) in the knowledge of God; the whole nature was seen as failed. Nobody, in spite of his virtues and capacities, could overcome the standing obstacles. With the incarnation of the Logos, the personal calling of God is realized in concrete form and, as a whole entity, becomes a historical presence "in the flesh" in the person of the theandric Christ. At the same time this Person incarnates the wholeness of man's acceptance of God's invitation to participate in the offered blessings. It is rather a renewal of God's invitation, addressed to many at every moment in the past through the Old Testament and now again in a new form.

Christ, in fact, is a new creation of God, a new *ktisis*. Because of this, he is exempt from the curse of Adam. Although "new," the Logos continues to be a free Person taken from the human race. His originality lies in the complete communion of the divine with the human nature. The fallen and distorted human nature, until now hostile to God, is recapitulated in Christ's person, and thus becomes a partaker of the divine nature (2 Pet. 1:4). This restoration is twofold: personal and universal or catholic. Therefore, any attitude, positive or negative, toward the calling of God is no longer a matter of nature but of the entire free choice of persons. Dionysius the Areopagite comments:

> The infinite goodness-philanthropy having truly participated in our human nature, sin excepted, and being identified with our fragility, with the unconfused and undamaged habit, it granted to us the same communion as being of the same race.[132]

[132]*The Ecclesiastical Hierarchy* 3 (PG 3.441).

The double cooperation God-man cannot be understood without also the presence of God's Spirit, because it is the Spirit who transfuses divine life and true liberty. He is working in all circumstances in time and space, particularly within God's family of redeemed people, that is, his church. Penetrating man's life through the sanctifying sacraments, the Spirit makes man a partaker of God's glory and enables a communion and dialogue with God which is open to spiritual appeals. There is no doubt that there exists a mystery in this operation, when "God hidden" (Isa. 45:15) enters in communion with the inner life of man with what Peter calls *ho kryptos tēs kardias anthropos* (1 Pet. 3:4). Of course, all these blessings must be understood in a communal and not in an individualistic manner. We all share the gifts of God. Man is saved with others, never separately. We are responsible, therefore, for the salvation of others and for all the universe.

Such an approach makes a Christian not an introverted individual but a creator who finds ways and means to help the expansion of truth—whose vocation is to influence, to transform the life around him, and to create a new culture in the process of expanding God's kingdom. Transformation of humanity depends both on God and man's creativity; it is not a utopia but the consequence of the descent and manifestation of the divine in earthly realities. Christ incarnate is Emmanuel, which means he remains with us and for us. It is not enough for men to master the cosmos; we must also transfigure it through prayer.

Orthodox spirituality is often accomplished thanks to monastic asceticism. Holiness is a vast area for Christians to influence the process of humanity. Each faithful believer is both an ecclesiastical and liturgical being, called to doxology, prayer, and *diaconia*. Christian optimism is not a naive expectation of a messianism—a futurology that is purely social with narrow visions and overstated slogans like progress, universal peace, and earthly paradise. What we feel above all is the permanent actuality of Christ's presence. When so much publicity is given to humanizing, what is meant? With what criteria and on what model is humanization achieved? Only the model Christ who became man without losing his divinity can incite to imitation and authentic human promotion.

This reflects, too, the ascending process of our life for better, otherworldly realities. We are, according to the fathers, in the process of becoming, since in the actual state we are not complete and perfect. Alienation from Christ's communion makes man unemancipated in reality: dehumanized, degraded, less human. Man's mystery is clarified only in the light of Christ's mystery. This implies a permanent God-man relationship. We cannot leave all the work to God to the exclusion of human activity. At the same time, it is not right to exclude and leave God in exile in heaven under the pretext that man will become self-sufficient, really free, and autonomous. In human nature there is a thirst and a natural ontological openness toward his very origins and roots based on the fact that he is created according to God's image. From his very nature man learns other values and realities than those on earth, those that are temporal and unstable. John of Damascus has given an excellent description of man when he describes him as "needing more explications."[133]

Man indeed bears the whole mystery of divine-humanity. Far from being idealization or triumphalism, it is the only answer to the tragic situation of the modern man who tries to find his true identity and his destiny in a chaotic and frustrated world.

The fathers were aware of the supreme importance of man's participation in the liturgical life and underlined its influence upon man's behavior. Thus Cyril of Jerusalem states:

> You will be armed not with perishable but with spiritual weapons. The paradise in which you will be planted is the soul's paradise, where you will be named with a name you did not have before. You were a catechumen until now but from now on you will be called a believer. From now on you will be transplanted among the olives of that paradise. Having been taken from a wild olive, you will be grafted on a good olive tree (Rom. 2:17–24). You will pass from sinfulness to righteousness, from defilement to purity. You will become part of the Holy Vine . . .[134]

A Christian's life is incoherent and inconsistent without his membership in the church, without abiding in this sacramental communion. For the church is the ambiance in which we achieve our union with God in this present earthly life. This union will be completed in the life hereafter, following the resurrection of the dead. It is impossible to understand Christ's salvation without the church,

[133]*Homilia in ficum arefactum* (PG 96.608).
[134]*Catechetical Lectures* 4.

for it is the church which generates and renews all those who enter it. Whatever we might need for our salvation, we will find only in the church. A Christian feels the power of divine grace acting upon him through the sacraments, the liturgical setting, and the whole spiritual order of the ecclesial life. As one lives this life, one attains an unshakeable conviction of the truth of one's faith in the church of Christ.

Living a Corporate Reality

A TRAGIC TYPE of Christianity prevails today when people live a natural or individualistic piety without a churchly life. It reminds one of a traveler who knows neither where he is going nor how to arrive at his destination. The aim of a man outside the liturgical life is a duality of thought and action. He thinks that he alone hears the angel's concert when in reality he hears only the voice of his own ego, his own distorted self.

The first fruit of membership within the ecclesiastical community is the broadening of the human personality through communal action. Outside, it is restricted to a narrow ego. My ego in the Liturgy finds many other egos. Thus I become more aware of myself as I find my place in the community, the church. This is not the achievement of an instant. It requires a slow process with waverings, hesitations, exaltations, moments of indifference, and the sacrifice of personal interests for the common good.

It is true that natural man often wants to go beyond himself, to break out of his imprisonment. But he only finds similar men suffering from the same agonies and perplexities. He cannot raise his head to heaven. Within the liturgical life he finds all the vital elements for his growth and progress in the sunshine of God's grace. This sunshine is sought in vain by nonsacramental efforts; even if man may display some qualities in this case, they are very atrophic and anemic. In a self-centered life, mutual correction is absent and koinonia is a falsified ethereal or sociological fellowship.

The stimulus provided by our own capacities is not sufficient to overcome the dominance of our carnal being. Just as our soul becomes hardened when nourished only by its own substance, so it becomes alive, creative, and dynamic when it is plunged in the Liturgy.

By including even the natural world as sharing the glory of the resurrection, Orthodox eucharistic theology shows the breadth of Christ's redemptive work. It wants to show that everything in crea-

114

tion is part of the universe, and that everything may be sanctified and not rejected as unworthy. Our respect is especially required for the body, the temple of the Spirit. It is the instrument of the unseen world within us. Man is the image of God, an *alter Christus.*

For this reason, the Liturgy, albeit a great mystery, is very human and comprehensible. It asks not only for our spiritual wants but contains a great many petitions dealing with earthly needs. There are prayers for the sick, for relief from insomnia, for water wells, for animals, for protection against tree diseases, for good weather, for fishermen that they may have a good catch. Our welfare, in the real sense of the word, is made up of many detailed factors. The church takes good care of every aspect and neglects nothing. We can understand why all these bodily and material elements find such a considerable place in a worship grounded in spirit and truth. Both aspects must be sanctified equally, because the whole of our human substance has to glorify God.

In other words, the faithful Christian lives with the church and upon the church. He relies upon the prayer and help of his fellows. The Epistle to the Hebrews warns against a separatistic conception of worship when it says "not neglecting to meet together, as is the habit of some, but encouraging one another" (Heb. 10:25). We find a similar statement in Ps. 78:52: "Then he led forth his people like sheep, and guided them in the wilderness like a flock." Here the equivalent of the Hebrew word for "flock," the Greek *synagog* as translated by the Septuagint, has been the subject of a sacramental and liturgical interpretation by Origen, the great doctor of the Alexandrian school. He finds here the real physiognomy of Christian worship. Meeting together means praying together, obtaining strength together from the same chalice and the same bread. Any departure from or abandoning of this fellowship leads one astray toward all the dangers and enemies of our souls, which are lying in wait to catch their victims.

> By holding these assemblies, we are maintaining the mystery of the flock. But if we neglect them, we follow the example of those sheep who run away from their companions. As a result, their enemies the wolves can attack and catch them, which is what we see in practice. But when a sheep stays with the flock, even if it is being attacked, it will resist attacks more easily. You see how many dangers beset the isolated sheep.

If we do not want to fall prey to the power of our adversities, let us
not abandon the assembly but be eager to meet and honor the day
of the resurrection of Christ, in order that the bones of Christ may
join the other bones, the nerves, the skin, the hair, the bowels. Forget not that you are the body of Christ, and it is necessary to be
assembled so that Christ cannot say "my bones have been disjoined"
(Ps. 22:14).[135]

We find this close relationship of Christians in various parts of
the Liturgy. Thus in the consecration prayer of St. Basil, we seek
grace that it may unite us with the Holy Spirit and through him
with all who are involved in the Eucharist. Communion is not just a
personal matter aimed at strengthening the spiritual life of the
separate members. It is not intended that they should remain separate, but that they may grow together and be one family and one
body, giving that wonderful unity in Christ: "Bring us together,
one to another, having participated in the one bread and the one
chalice, to the one communion of the Holy Spirit."

Thus we have corporate worship. We never pray alone, isolated.
We pray together with the vast throng of those who are the church
triumphant in heaven. This is immediately evident upon entering an
Orthodox church. The number of icons and frescoes is not a matter
of iconographic decoration or aesthetic beauty alone. Their presence aims at reminding the worshiper that in praying he is accompanied by all the souls who are now near the throne of the
Almighty. So we live a continuous and empirical intercommunion
between the two realities: the visible and the unseen, the church
militant and the church triumphant.

Holy Communion is closely related to a twofold reconciliation
taking place through a sincere private confession of sins. The idea,
apart from its disciplinary character, is that the Christian has to be
reconciled with God and with the community. His offences must be
cleared. Divine mercy and pardon will be accorded after the church
has been persuaded that he is a real penitent.

[135]Origen, *Analecta Sacra,* ed. J. Pitra, iii, 129.

The Impact of Liturgy

ST. PAUL WAS AMAZED at the mystery of Christ's incarnation: "Great indeed, we confess, is the mystery of our religion: He (God) was manifested in the flesh" (1 Tim. 3:16). Indeed, one must be exceedingly careful about how one dwells upon the human nature of Christ. One must not set him before the people as a man with the propensities of sin. He is the second Adam. The first Adam was created a pure sinless being without a taint of sin upon him. He was the image of God. He could fall, and he did fall because of his transgression. Because of sin his posterity was born with inherent propensities to disobedience. But Christ was the only-begotten Son of God. He took upon himself human nature and was tempted in all the ways that human nature could be tempted. One may even dare to say that he could have sinned. He was assailed with temptations in the wilderness, as Adam was assailed with temptations in Eden. He could have fallen, if he had wanted to. But not for one moment was there an evil propensity in him.

Spirituality is not an abstract idea, a vague mysticism. It is the work of God on earth in the life of Christ which explains the link and tells us how to be at home in both the world and the Spirit, or rather, how to regard them both as a single world of the Spirit. The forms of Christian spirituality are forms of grace which allow us to find God in freedom. The promised land of the human race is in God himself, and Christ is the Moses who has come to show us the way to reach it. He has placed before us once again the choice which was placed before Adam. We are shown the road to follow, and we are given the freedom to choose that road. This is the paradox of grace—a privilege and a burden. The more we postpone this choice the longer we are in spiritual exile. "Where there is no vision, the people perish" (Prov. 29:18, *KJV*).

The theological meaning of the transfiguration is to be found in its significance for successive ages of Christian life. It is best ap-

proached as an epitome of the meaning of the incarnation itself. To
the Christian, the historical man Jesus of Nazareth, though fully
one with humanity, has a significance far beyond that which is attached to any other member of the human race. In him, God is
made manifest. As he said: "We . . . beheld his glory," and added
that the glory was that "of the only Son of the Father" (John
1:14).

The eye of faith, therefore, sees all the words and deeds of Jesus
transfigured with a heavenly light. They are not merely significant
but deeply and ultimately significant. The divine command heard
at the transfiguration "This is my beloved Son . . . listen to him" is to
be understood as covering the whole gospel story. As Christ is
fully one with humanity, the vision of his glory is for us the pledge
of a destiny more satisfying than that of ordinary earthly existence
with its disappointments and frustrations. St. Paul was bold enough
to say that Christians themselves were being transfigured into the
same faith with all that it costs to reach that fulfillment. The Christian church in many lands can agree with this.

The paradoxes of Jesus and the inner relationship of liturgical
actions to the life of a believer are described by Gregory of
Nazianzus. Whatever happened in Christ's redeeming ministry for
the salvation of mankind is continuing in the sacramental life, thus
bestowing his grace:

He was born,
　but he was already begotten;
He issued from a woman,
　but she was a virgin . . .
He was wrapped in swaddling bands,
　but he removed the swaddling clothes of the grave when he rose
　　again.
He was laid in a manger,
　but he was glorified by angels, and proclaimed by a star,
　and worshipped by the Magi.
He had no form nor comeliness in the eyes of the Jews,
　but to David he was fairer than the children of men. And on the
　mountain he was bright as the lightning and became more
　luminous than the sun, initiating us into the mysteries of the
　future.
He was baptized as man,
　but he remitted sins as God.

He was tempted as man,
  but he conquered as God.
He hungered,
  but he fed thousands.
He thirsted,
  but he cried, "If any man thirst, let him come unto me and drink."
He was weary,
  but he is the peace of them that are sorrowful and heavy-laden.
He prays,
  but he hears prayer.
He weeps,
  but he puts an end to tears.
He asks where Lazarus was laid, for he was a man;
  and he raises Lazarus, for He is God . . .
As a sheep he is led to the slaughter,
  but he is the Shepherd of Israel and now of the whole world . . .
He is bruised and wounded,
  but he heals every disease and every infirmity.
He is lifted up and nailed to the tree,
  but by the tree of life he restores us . . .
He lays down his life,
  but he has the power to take it again; and the veil is rent, for the
  mysterious doors of heaven are opened; the rocks are cleft, the
  dead arise.
He dies,
  but he gives life, and by his death destroys death . . .
He is buried,
  but he rises again.
He goes down to hell,
  but he saves the damned.[136]

All feasts prepare Christians to receive Christ. During Advent, for
example, we sing in the Orthodox hymnography:

Christ is born, glorify Him.
Christ comes from heaven, welcome Him.
Christ is now on earth, go out to meet Him.

All that the church does during these days is intended to prepare
us worthily to meet Christ in the manger, to help us understand
this, and to live accordingly. Thus we penetrate the mystery of the
coming into flesh of God's only Son. We consider how the world
and man were created in and for him. We see his reflection and

[136]Gregory of Nazianzus, *Oratio* XXIX, 19, 20.

image in one another. In joy we remember the first gospel which God gives us about him immediately after our fall (Gen. 3:15). The best of Christmas is revealed when it enters into our personal lives. Clement of Alexandria long ago said: "Our whole life is one festival. Persuaded that God is with us, we cultivate our fields, praising, and we sail the seas hymning."

This is putting things in a good perspective. The Spirit of rejoicing, of kindness, of Christ, is not something which comes once a year, but it is the great treasure of one's whole life from the cradle to the grave and even beyond.

The ascension is not merely a spectacular sign of Christ's divine majesty; it also demonstrates the continuing victory of his ministry and of his followers. Whatever happens to him as head of the body also happens, by interpenetration or *perichoresis,* to the members of his body, namely, all who are baptized. The opening of the Book of Acts clearly demonstrates this. All that Jesus (the central figure of this book) began is still alive and at work, continuing what he has begun. What springs from this book is his triumph. To the highest place in heaven the Son of God has returned, bearing manhood with him. In his hands is still the imprint of the nails. His work was to go on, but it was to go on through his disciples. No longer was it to be limited to Palestine; they were to be his witness to the outermost parts of the earth.

Active faith dedicates all spheres of life and its gifts to God. Sacraments are a special form of worship; they are not only a sign of faith, but a means through which the Holy Spirit enacts its grace, which is voluntarily accepted.

The central sacrament is the Eucharist performed during the Divine Liturgy. Here, Christology and soteriology, the experiencing of the life and the sacrifice of Jesus Christ, his resurrection and Parousia, are united. At the same time, the Holy Eucharist strengthens the communicant in such a way that he is no longer what he was before—weak, fragile, hopeless, timid. For this reason, St. Basil of Caesarea strongly recommends frequent Communion as the only means of sustaining our weak nature.[137]

With regard to contemporary interest, especially that of young Christians, in intercommunion, we should beware of introducing

[137]*Letter* 243 (PG 32.484–85).

it too hastily. Without accepting the common teachings about the Lord's Supper, intercommunion would be a mechanical measure if not inconsistent faith and hypocrisy.

Concerning the difficulties of worship and prayer in a secular age, this age may be characterized as an attempt of man to gain independence from God, an attempt of some type of Promethean egoism, of titanism of the human mind. It is an age-old problem which has existed since the biblical fall of man. The result of secularism is the weakening of the so-called liturgical sense and the restriction of liturgical life to a minimum, even among Christians. The former continuous liturgical life is mostly reduced to occasional services.

Bitter and disappointed, contemporary man needs to find security in worship because he lives in the insecurity of the world and of his vacillating inner self. Should he seek worship, or should the worshiping church seek him out? Should worship change according to man's changing inner self and his nostalgia for escape from sin, or should worship stabilize his inner self, convert it to repentance, and consecrate his life and faith to union with Jesus Christ?

The present era has imposed many liturgical changes (even in traditional churches), mainly with a view to shortening the time of worship. In the charismatic era of the old church, creative freedom which allowed for liturgical improvisation reigned. But this was not arbitrary, individual whimsy. The churches know that it is impossible to dogmatize outer acts, gestures, and liturgical language. In striving to modernize worship, it is necessary to beware of senseless formalism, rationalistic formulations, doctrinization, and especially the play of fantasy and sensuality.

In conclusion, God does not need our prayers, but he needs the mutual prayer of believers in a dialogue of the spirit of love in the church. Mutual prayer is the blood of the church, and her breath is the praise of God.

As the fathers understood from the very beginning, the church is not just a window through which one sentimentally glimpses a part of heaven and the metaphysical world. Rather, it is the mystical ladder on which man ascends and God descends, so that a real ascent and descent (*anabasis* and *katabasis*) takes place, resulting in the blessed meeting between Creator and creature. Such an operation has a totally salutary effect upon man's life, ontologically and eschatologically.

Photius, patriarch of Constantinople (810-95), left us a wonderful analogy when he compared the saving action of the church to that of a ferryboat arriving from the celestial coast, conveying to all of us the divine compassion and overwhelming grace of God's philanthropy: *diaporthmeuei hēmin tēn ekeithen agathoeidē kai theian eumeneian.*[138]

[138]*Quaestiones Amphilochia* 111 (PG 101.656).

Are We Ready for a New Creed?

A NEW CONFESSION of faith appears at first sight a timely and legitimate question already preoccupying many churches in the West.[139] A precondition to this seems to be that such a text should be relevant and in complete harmony with the faith proclaimed by the undivided universal church of all times. This, however, is bound to provoke serious hesitations since a new confession of faith, formulated in the minimalistic form of a United Nations decision, will not be able, in spite of all good intention, to hide the existing disagreements. The reason for this is that in spite of the fact that many if not all Christians are using the same Nicene-Constantinopolitan Creed, we are still divided and subdivided. A mere proclamation of our common faith, however venerable and respectable in itself, is simply not enough to eliminate the existing doctrinal tensions and reduce the degree of our divisions.

Let us imagine what might happen in case of such a new text. Each particular church will choose what is most essential and will underline what best suits its own doctrine and identity. It will try to show as indispensable all elements special to it, insisting that its priorities be included above anything else in such a credo. Another danger lies in the possibility that each of the faithful within a particular church might give his own interpretation to the contents of the new creed, since a new proclamation of faith is bound to reflect the current stream of belief inside the constituency of this church. There is no doubt that such a text will sooner or later betray a *complexio oppositorum* with all kinds of misgivings, which would show the fragility of our enterprise.

More than all others, the Orthodox are ready to share a common statement of faith, but experience shows that more work has

[139]See the text of "Towards a Confession of the Common Faith, Faith and Order Paper 100, *The Ecumenical Review* 32 (July 1980): 309–17. See also my article, "Common and Uncommon Faith," *The Ecumenical Review* 32 (October 1980): 396–409.

to be done before this stage can be reached. As things stand today, little progress has been made in the Faith and Order, World Council of Churches' discussions where the methodology adopted is based on a *kat' oikonomian* solution and compromise agreements.

Facing this situation, the Orthodox presence in the ecumenical movement does not consist in reducing the speed for the unity negotiations, but in recalling questions that touch on the essentials of our common faith, for which the early fathers and the ecumenical councils have fought. Of course, the climate today is more favorable than before for elucidating obscure positions and persistent misunderstandings. Still, a deeper acquaintance with the language and theological thinking of the Orthodox is needed if the historical development of doctrines confronting the East and the West is to be rightly understood.

One safe and sure way might be to start with common statements or declarations concerning common issues—human religious issues and vital problems of a healthy church or society. Such starting points may lead little by little to deeper doctrinal convergences. After all, such a holistic approach will show to what extent the questions that face us are indivisible and interrelated. If convergences are achieved on spiritual, moral, and human issues, we can proceed to further steps, which may bring us nearer and nearer to each other in our searching. Nobody is opposed to a common witness before a world that is threatened by agnosticism, institutionalized atheism, syncretism, or nihilism—all of which penetrate society, endangering all Christians and humankind as a whole. Such a progressive procedure, confident of God's guidance for speaking the truth courageously (the Pauline *parhesia*), would open new possibilities and chances for joined action and confession of the Christ as Redeemer, the only hope and unique Savior and *Kyrios* of a humanity frustrated with its own idols.

Let me now come to the inner connection of an eventual new confession with the faith proclaimed in the ancient Creed. As is well known, all classical creeds enjoyed the approbation and consent of church delegates coming from the same undivided one church either of the East or of the West, excluding all heterodoxical participation. Such a unanimous statement on faith served not only the pressing needs of the Christians of those times, but also the need for more permanent and unmovable texts clearly explaining the articles of faith for all times for the church of today and of tomorrow. There are two essential features in such a confession of faith; we can label these features as synchronic and diachronic. The first corresponds to the emerging doctrinal needs of the church at a certain historical moment constituting a reaction to an alarming situation of a given church in time and space. Such was the framework of the first Nicene Creed of 325 against the threat of Arianism. The second presupposes the church to be, in the plan of divine economy, the arch of believers for all times beyond the limitations of history, and thus it anticipates the future and forthcoming dangers. Heresy was not a unique phenomenon of the primitive church. Throughout its life the church had to face again and again Crypto-Arians, Neo-Arians, Gnostics, Monophysites, and Monothelites, all of whom under different cover distorted inherited truth and apostolic teaching.

Such being the status of a confession (a text embodying *nova et vetera*), let us turn our attention to how a new confession—formed by the participation of many Christian families most of which issued from the Reformation, showing fundamental disagreements on matters of faith plus attributing a different value and authority to a creed—can be reached. It must, to be sure, be in complete agreement with the same faith and teaching which an unbroken tradition of the church of all times has transmitted to us. I put the question: how can such an incoherent, heterogenous assembly produce, for the sake of unity, a satisfying text?

For the sake of clarity, let me again remind you that the Nicene Creed was dictated by needs of faith which challenged the bishops who gathered together in 325, all of whom belonged to the same faith. A symphony of opinion and belief already prevailed. That text, therefore, was a real *homologia*, that is, it was *homou*, "together," without discord or disagreement. It is this same *homologia* that the Reformed churches stick to, inserting the Nicene Creed into their worship in order to prove their basic Christian credibility. Thus, the most doctrinally incoherent churches are using this creedal text until this day in spite of their numerous divergencies in theology and praxis.

Because of this I conclude that one should not overstress the fact that a common text is accepted by different churches as a confessional form of their faith. If this text has no impact upon the whole

life of the church in question, if it does not pervade the whole structure, discipline, ethic, spirituality, and daily belief of each member,
it risks remaining a foreign body inside this church, without any
intimate and organic relation to its life. This leads me to one last
observation, this one regarding our position toward the Roman
Catholic Church. Recently (June 1981), the Nicene Creed in its
original Greek form was read without the famous controversial
Filioque by the pope in Rome during the Pentecostal manifestations.
Everybody rejoiced and saluted this as a good start for a return to
the ancient faith of the undivided church. Without underestimating
the value of this gesture of the bishop of Rome, I do not hesitate
to consider it as an isolated goodwill token as long as it is not
accompanied by a deeper and substantial change in the Roman
theology which restores pneumatology in all sectors of church life.
Sporadic acts or documents remain weak unless they are followed
by sincere efforts for a wider revision of many distorted attitudes.
One wishes that the whole of Catholic theology be plunged again
into the doctrine of the Holy Spirit, the Paraclete, "Lord and life-
giving," harmonizing and detecting the orthodoxy and healthy life
of the Christian community on the whole and not only regarding
specific details and cases.

As we can see, ancient creeds were not instant compositions of
texts during a synod. Rather, they were the outcome of a long
process of faith, deeply permeated in the whole life—religious,
disciplinary, liturgical, theological—of the entire church. They were
expressing what already had become a living reality or what commonly is called tradition. This living tradition in the church was
consistent throughout history but was made known to each genera-
tion in terms understandable to the people. Of course, a new language always is needed. But there is a difference between talking
about Jesus in a new way and talking about a new Jesus.

Epilogue

IT APPEARED NECESSARY to the Second Ecumenical Council to re-
form and complete the first seven articles of the precedent Creed
(notably to dismantle new heresies which had cropped up since
the First Council) by adding, subtracting, and changing a good
number of things which were then incorporated into the original
version. The most important are the following: "maker of heaven
and earth," against the Marcionites, the Manichaeans, and especially
Hermogenes, all of whom proclaimed matter to be eternal; "before
all ages" (eternally begotten), against Sabellius, Marcellus of
Ancyra, Photinus of Sirmium, and Eunomius, who thought otherwise; "[born] of the Holy Spirit and the Virgin Mary," against the
Apollinarists; "was crucified for us under Pontius Pilate . . . and
was buried," likewise against the Apollinarists and to complete the
relevant Nicene article.

In this way the task of the Second Ecumenical Council, notably
its definition of doctrine which included the basic doctrine on the
Holy Trinity, was achieved. Thus was perfected, generally speaking,
the firm doctrinal groundwork laid by the First Ecumenical Council, the whole doctrinal structure of the primitive church. In this
lay the prime importance of the first two ecumenical councils which,
together with the following five, "spoke forth with divine inspiration" under the guidance of the Holy Spirit. They set forth authentic articles of faith, immutable, binding on all Christians of every
age. "Whatever is accomplished in the holy councils of the bishops
is in accordance with divine will," to quote the words of Constantine
the Great.[140]

Thus completed, a seal was set on the "Creed of Nicaea-
Constantinople," of which the Orthodox Church sings in its hymnography: "Bringing together all the science of the soul and meeting
under the wings of the Holy Spirit, the venerable fathers outlined

[140]Eusebius, *Life of Constantine* III, 20 (PG 20.1080).

the blessed and venerable Creed in divine terms; in it they teach most clearly the Verb to be cooriginal with the Begotten and most truly consubstantial, thereby manifestly following the teachings of the apostles . . . having clearly received the revelation of these things from above and being thus enlightened, they set forth a divinely taught ordinance."[141]

The remembrance of the Creed gives all Christians an opportunity to rededicate themselves to the spirit of conciliarity that inspires our church. The church itself is a permanent council. A council is an event of the Holy Spirit. It is a new Pentecost, because the Spirit of Pentecost is at work in the ecumenical council to guide the fathers in their deliberations, decisions, and overall task, which is to defend and proclaim inviolate the faith.

We glory in the Creed of faith, which was established and proclaimed by the Second Ecumenical Council. At the same time we need to constantly recommit ourselves to the Spirit that inspired the fathers of this council and to the faith proclaimed by them. We need to recommit ourselves likewise to the faith in the one Holy Spirit, who is Lord and is worshiped and glorified with the Father and the Son. He is the Paraclete, the Counselor and the Comforter who inspires and instills life into the one holy catholic and apostolic church.

[141]Doxastikon of Ainoi, Matins of the feast.